FEB. 2013

Test Results for Mobile Device Acquisition Tool:
Device Seizure v5.0 build 4582.15907

NCJ 241153

Greg Ridgeway

Acting Director, National Institute of Justice

This report was prepared for the National Institute of Justice, U.S. Department of Justice, by the Office of Law Enforcement Standards of the National Institute of Standards and Technology under Interagency Agreement 2003–IJ–R–029.

The National Institute of Justice is a component of the Office of Justice Programs, which also includes the Bureau of Justice Assistance, the Bureau of Justice Statistics, the Office of Juvenile Justice and Delinquency Prevention, and the Office for Victims of Crime.

February 2013

Test Results for Mobile Device Acquisition Tool:
Device Seizure v5.0 build 4582.15907

National Institute of
Standards and Technology
U.S. Department of Commerce

Contents

Introduction

The Computer Forensics Tool Testing (CFTT) program is a joint project of the National Institute of Justice (NIJ), the Department of Homeland Security Science and Technology Directorate (DHS S&T), and the National Institute of Standards and Technology Office of Law Enforcement Standards (OLES) and Information Technology Laboratory (ITL). CFTT is supported by other organizations, including the Federal Bureau of Investigation, the U.S. Department of Defense Cyber Crime Center, the U.S. Internal Revenue Service Criminal Investigation Division Electronic Crimes Program, the U.S. Department of Homeland Security's Bureau of Immigration and Customs Enforcement, U.S. Customs and Border Protection, and U.S. Secret Service, the Naval Postgraduate School, the National White Collar Crime Center, the Commodity Futures Trading Commission, the U.S. Postal Service, and the Securities and Exchange Commission. The objective of the CFTT program is to provide measurable assurance to practitioners, researchers, and other applicable users that the tools used in computer forensics investigations provide accurate results. Accomplishing this requires the development of specifications and test methods for computer forensics tools and subsequent testing of specific tools against those specifications.

Test results provide the information necessary for developers to improve tools, for users to make informed choices, and for the legal community and others to understand the tools' capabilities. The CFTT approach to testing computer forensic tools is based on well-recognized methodologies for conformance and quality testing. The specifications and test methods posted on the CFTT Web site (http://www.cftt.nist.gov/) are available for review and comment by the computer forensics community.

This document reports the results from testing Device Seizure version 5.0 build 4582.15907 against the *Smart Phone Tool Test Assertions and Test Plan*, available at the CFTT Web site (www.cftt.nist.gov/mobile_devices.htm).

Test results from other tools and the CFTT tool methodology can be found on NIJ's computer forensics tool testing Web

page, http://www.ojp.usdoj.gov/nij/topics/technology/electronic–crime/cftt.htm.

How to Read This Report

This report is divided into five sections. The first section is a summary of the results from the test runs. This section is sufficient for most readers to assess the suitability of the tool for the intended use. The remaining sections of the report describe how the tests were conducted, discuss any anomalies that were encountered, and provide documentation of test case run details that support the report summary. Section 2 gives justification for the selection of test cases from the set of possible cases defined in the test plan for Smart Phone forensic tools. The test cases are selected, in general, on the basis of features offered by the tool. Section 3 describes in more depth any anomalies summarized in the first section. Section 4 lists hardware and software used to run the test cases. Section 5 contains a description of each test case run. The description of each test run lists all test assertions used in the test case, the expected result, and the actual result. Please refer to the vendor's owner manual for guidance on using the tool.

Test Results for Mobile Device Data Acquisition Tool

Tool Tested:	Device Seizure
Version:	5 build 4582.15907
Run Environment:	Microsoft Windows XP v5.1.2600
Supplier:	Paraben Corporation
Address:	21690 Red Rum Drive Ste 137 Ashburn, VA 20147
Tel:	801–796–0944
Fax:	517–918–4054
WWW:	http://www.paraben.com

1   Results Summary

Device Seizure is designed for logical and physical acquisitions, data analysis, and report management from mobile phones, Smart Phones, and Subscriber Identity Modules (SIMs).

The tool was tested for its ability to acquire active and deleted data from the internal memory of mobile devices and SIMs. Except for the following anomalies, the tool acquired all supported data objects completely and accurately for all six mobile devices tested.

Device connectivity:
- Connectivity to the mobile device was not established. (Nokia 6350)
- Connectivity during the acquisition ended in errors. (HTC Thunderbolt)

Subscriber and equipment related information:
- Subscriber related information was not reported. (iPhone4 GSM, iPhone4 CDMA, Palm Pre2)
- Equipment-related information was not reported. (iPhone4 CDMA, Palm Pre2)

Personal Information Management (PIM) data:
- Calendar entries and memos were not reported. (HTC Thunderbolt, Palm Pre2)
- Address book entries were not reported. (Palm Pre2)
- Graphics files associated with contacts were not reported. (iPhone4 GSM, BlackBerry Torch, iPhone4 CDMA)

Call logs:
- Call log data: incoming, outgoing, and missed calls were not acquired. (Palm Pre2)
- Missed calls were categorized as Incoming. (iPhone4 GSM, iPhone4 CDMA)

Acquisition of SMS messages:
- Unread text messages were not assigned a status. (iPhone4 GSM, iPhone4 CDMA)
- SMS messages were not reported. (Palm Pre2)

Acquisition of MMS messages:
- MMS messages were not reported. (Palm Pre2)
- MMS attachments: audio, graphic, and video files were not reported. (BlackBerry Torch)
- MMS attachments: audio files were not reported. (iPhone4 GSM, iPhone4 CDMA)
- The textual portion of MMS messages was not reported. (iPhone4 CDMA)

Acquisition of stand-alone files:
- Audio and video files were not reported. (iPhone4 GSM, iPhone4 CDMA)
- Audio, video and graphic files were not reported. (BlackBerry Torch, HTC Thunderbolt, Palm Pre2)

Application-related data:
- Application-related data (e.g., Quickoffice documents) were not acquired. (HTC Thunderbolt, Palm Pre2)

Internet-related data:
- Bookmarks and visited sites were not reported. (Palm Pre2)

Non-ASCII characters:
- Text messages containing the non-ASCII character 'é' were reported as '|'. (BlackBerry Torch)
- Contact entries containing Chinese characters were not reported. (BlackBerry Torch)

Refer to sections 3.1–3.10 for additional details.

2 Test Case Selection

Test cases used to test mobile device acquisition tools are defined in *Smart Phone Tool Test Assertions and Test Plan Version 1.0*. To test a tool, test cases are selected from the *Test Plan* document on the basis of features offered by the tool. Not all test cases or test assertions are appropriate for all tools. There is a core set of base cases that are executed for every tool tested. Tool features guide the selection of additional test cases. If a given tool implements a given feature, then the test cases linked to that feature are run. Tables 1a–1f list the test cases available in Device Seizure. Tables 2a–2f list the test cases not available in Device Seizure.

Table 1a: Selected Test Cases (iPhone4 GSM)

Supported Optional Feature	Cases Selected for Execution
Base cases	SPT-01, SPT-02, SPT-03, SPT-04, SPT-05, SPT-06, SPT-07, SPT-08, SPT-09, SPT-10, SPT-12, SPT-13
Acquire SIM memory over supported interfaces	SPT-14

Supported Optional Feature	Cases Selected for Execution
(e.g., PC/SC reader).	
Attempt acquisition of a nonsupported SIM.	SPT-15
Begin SIM acquisition and interrupt connectivity by interface disengagement.	SPT-16
Acquire SIM memory and review reported subscriber and equipment related information (i.e., SPN, ICCID, IMSI, MSISDN).	SPT-17
Acquire SIM memory and review reported Abbreviated Dialing Numbers (ADN).	SPT-18
Acquire SIM memory and review reported Last Numbers Dialed (LND).	SPT-19
Acquire SIM memory, and review reported text messages (SMS, EMS).	SPT-20
Acquire SIM memory and review recoverable deleted text messages (SMS, EMS).	SPT-21
Acquire SIM memory and review reported location-related data (i.e., LOCI, GPRSLOCI).	SPT-22
Acquire SIM memory by selecting a combination of supported data elements.	SPT-23
Acquire mobile device internal memory, and review reported data via supported/generated report formats.	SPT-24
Acquire mobile device internal memory, and review reported data via the preview pane.	SPT-25
Acquire SIM memory, and review reported data via supported/generated report formats.	SPT-26
Acquire SIM memory and review reported data via the preview pane.	SPT-27
Attempt acquisition of a password-protected SIM.	SPT-28
After a successful mobile device internal memory, alter the case file via third-party means and attempt to reopen the case.	SPT-29
After a successful SIM acquisition, alter the case file via third-party means, and attempt to reopen the case.	SPT-30
Acquire mobile device internal memory and review data containing non-ASCII characters.	SPT-33
Acquire SIM memory and review data containing non-ASCII characters.	SPT-34
Begin acquisition on a PIN-protected SIM to determine if the tool provides an accurate count of the remaining number of PIN attempts and if the PIN attempts are decremented when entering an incorrect value.	SPT-35
Begin acquisition on a SIM whose PIN attempts have been exhausted to determine if the tool provides an accurate count of the remaining number of PUK attempts and if the PUK attempts are decremented when entering an incorrect value.	SPT-36

Supported Optional Feature	Cases Selected for Execution
Acquire mobile device internal memory and review hash values for vendor-supported data objects.	SPT-38
Acquire SIM memory and review hash values for vendor supported data objects.	SPT-39

Table 2a: Omitted Test Cases (iPhone4 GSM)

Unsupported Optional Feature	Cases Omitted / Not Executed
Acquire mobile device internal memory and review application-related data (i.e., Word documents, spreadsheet, presentation documents).	SPT-11
Perform a physical acquisition and review data output for readability.	SPT-31
Perform a physical acquisition and review reports for recoverable/deleted data.	SPT-32
Perform a stand-alone mobile device internal memory acquisition and review the status flags for text messages present on the SIM.	SPT-37
Acquire mobile device internal memory and review data containing GPS longitude and latitude coordinates.	SPT-40

Table 1b: Selected Test Cases (BlackBerry Torch)

Supported Optional Feature	Cases Selected for Execution
Base cases	SPT-01, SPT-02, SPT-03, SPT-04, SPT-05, SPT-06, SPT-07, SPT-08, SPT-09, SPT-10, SPT-12, SPT-13
Acquire SIM memory over supported interfaces (e.g., PC/SC reader).	SPT-14
Attempt acquisition of a nonsupported SIM.	SPT-15
Begin SIM acquisition and interrupt connectivity by interface disengagement.	SPT-16
Acquire SIM memory and review reported Abbreviated Dialing Numbers (ADN).	SPT-18
Acquire SIM memory and review reported Last Numbers Dialed (LND).	SPT-19
Acquire SIM memory and review reported text messages (SMS, EMS).	SPT-20
Acquire SIM memory, and review recoverable/deleted text messages (SMS, EMS).	SPT-21
Acquire SIM memory and review reported location-related data (i.e., LOCI, GPRSLOCI).	SPT-22
Acquire SIM memory by selecting a combination of supported data elements.	SPT-23
Acquire mobile device internal memory and review reported data via supported generated report formats.	SPT-24
Acquire mobile device internal memory and review reported	SPT-25

Supported Optional Feature	Cases Selected for Execution
data via the preview pane.	
Acquire SIM memory and review reported data via supported generated report formats.	SPT-26
Acquire SIM memory and review reported data via the preview pane.	SPT-27
Attempt acquisition of a password-protected SIM.	SPT-28
After a successful mobile device internal memory, alter the case file via third-party means and attempt to reopen the case.	SPT-29
After a successful SIM acquisition, alter the case file via third-party means and attempt to reopen the case.	SPT-30
Acquire mobile device internal memory and review data containing non-ASCII characters.	SPT-33
Acquire SIM memory and review data containing non-ASCII characters.	SPT-34
Begin acquisition on a PIN protected SIM to determine if the tool provides an accurate count of the remaining number of PIN attempts and if the PIN attempts are decremented when entering an incorrect value.	SPT-35
Begin acquisition on a SIM whose PIN attempts have been exhausted to determine if the tool provides an accurate count of the remaining number of PUK attempts and if the PUK attempts are decremented when entering an incorrect value.	SPT-36
Acquire mobile device internal memory and review hash values for vendor supported data objects.	SPT-38
Acquire SIM memory and review hash values for vendor supported data objects.	SPT-39

Table 2b: Omitted Test Cases (BlackBerry Torch)

Unsupported Optional Feature	Cases Omitted / Not Executed
Acquire mobile device internal memory and review application-related data (i.e., Word documents, spreadsheet, presentation documents).	SPT-11
Acquire SIM memory and review reported subscriber and equipment-related information (i.e., SPN, ICCID, IMSI, MSISDN).	SPT-17
Perform a physical acquisition and review data output for readability.	SPT-31
Perform a physical acquisition and review reports for recoverable/ deleted data.	SPT-32
Perform a stand-alone mobile device internal memory acquisition and review the status flags for text messages present on the SIM.	SPT-37
Acquire mobile device internal memory and review data containing GPS longitude and latitude coordinates.	SPT-40

Table 1c: Selected Test Cases (Nokia 6350)

Supported Optional Feature	Cases Selected for Execution
Base cases	SPT-01,
Acquire SIM memory over supported interfaces (e.g., PC/SC reader).	SPT-14
Attempt acquisition of a nonsupported SIM.	SPT-15
Begin SIM acquisition, and interrupt connectivity by interface disengagement.	SPT-16
Acquire SIM memory, and review reported subscriber and equipmentrelated information (i.e., SPN, ICCID, IMSI, MSISDN).	SPT-17
Acquire SIM memory, and review reported Abbreviated Dialing Numbers (ADN).	SPT-18
Acquire SIM memory, and review reported Last Numbers Dialed (LND).	SPT-19
Acquire SIM memory, and review reported text messages (SMS, EMS).	SPT-20
Acquire SIM memory, and review recoverable/deleted text messages (SMS, EMS).	SPT-21
Acquire SIM memory, and review reported location-related data (i.e., LOCI, GPRSLOCI).	SPT-22
Acquire SIM memory by selecting a combination of supported data elements.	SPT-23
Acquire SIM memory, and review reported data via supported generated report formats.	SPT-26
Acquire SIM memory, and review reported data via the preview pane.	SPT-27
Attempt acquisition of a password-protected SIM.	SPT-28
After a successful SIM acquisition, alter the case file via third-party means and attempt to reopen the case.	SPT-30
Acquire SIM memory, and review data containing non-ASCII characters.	SPT-34
Begin acquisition on a PIN-protected SIM to determine if the tool provides an accurate count of the remaining number of PIN attempts and if the PIN attempts are decremented when entering an incorrect value.	SPT-35
Begin acquisition on a SIM whose PIN attempts have been exhausted to determine if the tool provides an accurate count of the remaining number of PUK attempts and if the PUK attempts are decremented when entering an incorrect value.	SPT-36
Acquire SIM memory, and review hash values for vendor supported data objects.	SPT-39

Table 2c: Omitted Test Cases (Nokia 6350)

Unsupported Optional Feature	Cases Omitted / Not Executed
Attempt internal memory acquisition of a nonsupported mobile device.	SPT-02
Begin mobile device internal memory acquisition and interrupt connectivity by interface disengagement.	SPT-03
Acquire mobile device internal memory and review reported data via the preview pane or generated reports for readability.	SPT-04

Unsupported Optional Feature	Cases Omitted / Not Executed
Acquire mobile device internal memory and review reported subscriber and equipment related information (e.g., IMEI/MEID/ESN, MSISDN).	SPT-05
Acquire mobile device internal memory and review reported PIM-related data.	SPT-06
Acquire mobile device internal memory and review reported call logs.	SPT-07
Acquire mobile device internal memory and review reported text messages.	SPT-08
Acquire mobile device internal memory and review reported MMS multi-media-related data (i.e., text, audio, graphics, video).	SPT-09
Acquire mobile device internal memory and review reported stand-alone multi-media data (i.e., audio, graphics, video).	SPT-10
Acquire mobile device internal memory and review application-related data (i.e., Word documents, spreadsheet, presentation documents).	SPT-11
Acquire mobile device internal memory and review Internet-related data (i.e., bookmarks, visited sites.	SPT-12
Acquire mobile device internal memory by selecting a combination of supported data elements.	SPT-13
Acquire mobile device internal memory and review reported data via supported generated report formats.	SPT-24
Acquire mobile device internal memory and review reported data via the preview pane.	SPT-25
After a successful mobile device internal memory, alter the case file via third-party means and attempt to reopen the case.	SPT-29
Perform a physical acquisition and review data output for readability.	SPT-31
Perform a physical acquisition and review reports for recoverable deleted data.	SPT-32
Acquire mobile device internal memory and review data containing non-ASCII characters.	SPT-33
Perform a stand-alone mobile device internal memory acquisition and review the status flags for text messages present on the SIM.	SPT-37
Acquire mobile device internal memory and review hash values for vendor supported data objects.	SPT-38
Acquire mobile device internal memory and review data containing GPS longitude and latitude coordinates.	SPT-40

Table 1d: Selected Test Cases (iPhone4 CDMA)

Unsupported Optional Feature	Cases Omitted / Not Executed
Base cases	SPT-01, SPT-02, SPT-03, SPT-04, SPT-05, SPT-06, SPT-07, SPT-

Unsupported Optional Feature	Cases Omitted / Not Executed
	08, SPT-09, SPT-10, SPT-12, SPT-13
Acquire mobile device internal memory and review reported data via supported generated report formats.	SPT-24
Acquire mobile device internal memory and review reported data via the preview pane.	SPT-25
After a successful mobile device internal memory, alter the case file via third-party means and attempt to reopen the case.	SPT-29
Acquire mobile device internal memory and review data containing non-ASCII characters.	SPT-33
Acquire mobile device internal memory and review hash values for vendor supported data objects.	SPT-38

Table 2d: Omitted Test Cases (iPhone4 CDMA)

Unsupported Optional Feature	Cases Omitted / Not Executed
Acquire mobile device internal memory and review application-related data (i.e., Word documents, spreadsheet, presentation documents).	SPT-11
Acquire SIM memory over supported interfaces (e.g., PC/SC reader).	SPT-14
Attempt acquisition of a nonsupported SIM.	SPT-15
Begin SIM acquisition and interrupt connectivity by interface disengagement.	SPT-16
Acquire SIM memory and review reported subscriber and equipment related information (i.e., SPN, ICCID, IMSI, MSISDN).	SPT-17
Acquire SIM memory and review reported Abbreviated Dialing Numbers (ADN).	SPT-18
Acquire SIM memory and review reported Last Numbers Dialed (LND).	SPT-19
Acquire SIM memory and review reported text messages (SMS, EMS).	SPT-20
Acquire SIM memory and review recoverable/deleted text messages (SMS, EMS).	SPT-21
Acquire SIM memory and review reported location-related data (i.e., LOCI, GPRSLOCI).	SPT-22
Acquire SIM memory by selecting a combination of supported data elements.	SPT-23
Acquire SIM memory and review reported data via supported generated report formats.	SPT-26
Acquire SIM memory and review reported data via the preview pane.	SPT-27
Attempt acquisition of a password-protected SIM.	SPT-28
After a successful SIM acquisition, alter the case file via third-party means and attempt to reopen the case.	SPT-30
Perform a physical acquisition and review data output for readability.	SPT-31
Perform a physical acquisition and review reports for recoverable	SPT-32

Unsupported Optional Feature	Cases Omitted / Not Executed
deleted data.	
Acquire SIM memory and review data containing non-ASCII characters.	SPT-34
Begin acquisition on a PIN protected SIM to determine if the tool provides an accurate count of the remaining number of PIN attempts and if the PIN attempts are decremented when entering an incorrect value.	SPT-35
Begin acquisition on a SIM whose PIN attempts have been exhausted to determine if the tool provides an accurate count of the remaining number of PUK attempts and if the PUK attempts are decremented when entering an incorrect value.	SPT-36
Perform a stand-alone mobile device internal memory acquisition and review the status flags for text messages present on the SIM.	SPT-37
Acquire SIM memory and review hash values for vendor supported data objects.	SPT-39
Acquire mobile device internal memory and review data containing GPS longitude and latitude coordinates.	SPT-40

Table 1e: Selected Test Cases (HTC Thunderbolt)

Supported Optional Feature	Cases Selected for Execution
Base cases	SPT-01, SPT-02, SPT-03, SPT-04, SPT-05, SPT-06, SPT-07, SPT-08, SPT-09, SPT-10, SPT-11, SPT-12, SPT-13
Acquire mobile device internal memory and review reported data via supported generated report formats.	SPT-24
Acquire mobile device internal memory and review reported data via the preview pane.	SPT-25
After a successful mobile device internal memory, alter the case file via third-party means and attempt to reopen the case.	SPT-29
Acquire mobile device internal memory and review data containing non-ASCII characters.	SPT-33
Acquire mobile device internal memory and review hash values for vendor supported data objects.	SPT-38

Table 2e: Omitted Test Cases (HTC Thunderbolt)

Unsupported Optional Feature	Cases Omitted / Not Executed
Acquire SIM memory over supported interfaces (e.g., PC/SC reader).	SPT-14
Attempt acquisition of a nonsupported SIM.	SPT-15

Unsupported Optional Feature	Cases Omitted / Not Executed
Begin SIM acquisition and interrupt connectivity by interface disengagement.	SPT-16
Acquire SIM memory and review reported subscriber and equipment related information (i.e., SPN, ICCID, IMSI, MSISDN).	SPT-17
Acquire SIM memory and review reported Abbreviated Dialing Numbers (ADN).	SPT-18
Acquire SIM memory and review reported Last Numbers Dialed (LND).	SPT-19
Acquire SIM memory and review reported text messages (SMS, EMS).	SPT-20
Acquire SIM memory and review recoverable deleted text messages (SMS, EMS).	SPT-21
Acquire SIM memory and review reported location-related data (i.e., LOCI, GPRSLOCI).	SPT-22
Acquire SIM memory by selecting a combination of supported data elements.	SPT-23
Acquire SIM memory and review reported data via supported generated report formats.	SPT-26
Acquire SIM memory and review reported data via the preview pane.	SPT-27
Attempt acquisition of a password-protected SIM.	SPT-28
After a successful SIM acquisition, alter the case file via third-party means and attempt to reopen the case.	SPT-30
Perform a physical acquisition and review data output for readability.	SPT-31
Perform a physical acquisition and review reports for recoverable deleted data.	SPT-32
Acquire SIM memory and review data containing non-ASCII characters.	SPT-34
Begin acquisition on a PIN protected SIM to determine if the tool provides an accurate count of the remaining number of PIN attempts and if the PIN attempts are decremented when entering an incorrect value.	SPT-35
Begin acquisition on a SIM whose PIN attempts have been exhausted to determine if the tool provides an accurate count of the remaining number of PUK attempts and if the PUK attempts are decremented when entering an incorrect value.	SPT-36
Perform a stand-alone mobile device internal memory acquisition and review the status flags for text messages present on the SIM.	SPT-37
Acquire SIM memory and review hash values for vendor-supported data objects.	SPT-39
Acquire mobile device internal memory and review data containing GPS longitude and latitude coordinates.	SPT-40

Table 1f: Selected Test Cases (Palm Pre2)

Supported Optional Feature	Cases Selected for Execution
Base cases	SPT-01, SPT-02, SPT-03, SPT-04, SPT-

Supported Optional Feature	Cases Selected for Execution
	05, SPT-06, SPT-07, SPT-08, SPT-09, SPT-10, SPT-11, SPT-12, SPT-13
Acquire mobile device internal memory and review reported data via supported generated report formats.	SPT-24
Acquire mobile device internal memory and review reported data via the preview pane.	SPT-25
After a successful mobile device internal memory, alter the case file via third-party means and attempt to reopen the case.	SPT-29
Acquire mobile device internal memory and review hash values for vendor supported data objects.	SPT-38

Table 2f: Omitted Test Cases (Palm Pre2)

Unsupported Optional Feature	Cases Omitted / Not Executed
Acquire SIM memory over supported interfaces (e.g., PC/SC reader).	SPT-14
Attempt acquisition of a nonsupported SIM.	SPT-15
Begin SIM acquisition and interrupt connectivity by interface disengagement.	SPT-16
Acquire SIM memory and review reported subscriber and equipment related information (i.e., SPN, ICCID, IMSI, MSISDN).	SPT-17
Acquire SIM memory and review reported Abbreviated Dialing Numbers (ADN).	SPT-18
Acquire SIM memory and review reported Last Numbers Dialed (LND).	SPT-19
Acquire SIM memory and review reported text messages (SMS, EMS).	SPT-20
Acquire SIM memory and review recoverable deleted text messages (SMS, EMS).	SPT-21
Acquire SIM memory and review reported location-related data (i.e., LOCI, GPRSLOCI).	SPT-22
Acquire SIM memory by selecting a combination of supported data elements.	SPT-23
Acquire SIM memory and review reported data via supported generated report formats.	SPT-26
Acquire SIM memory and review reported data via the preview pane.	SPT-27
Attempt acquisition of a password-protected SIM.	SPT-28
After a successful SIM acquisition, alter the case file via third-party means and attempt to reopen the case.	SPT-30
Perform a physical acquisition and review data output for readability.	SPT-31
Perform a physical acquisition and review reports for recoverable deleted data.	SPT-32
Acquire mobile device internal memory and review data containing non-ASCII characters.	SPT-33

Unsupported Optional Feature	Cases Omitted / Not Executed
Acquire SIM memory and review data containing non-ASCII characters.	SPT-34
Begin acquisition on a PIN protected SIM to determine if the tool provides an accurate count of the remaining number of PIN attempts and if the PIN attempts are decremented when entering an incorrect value.	SPT-35
Begin acquisition on a SIM whose PIN attempts have been exhausted to determine if the tool provides an accurate count of the remaining number of PUK attempts and if the PUK attempts are decremented when entering an incorrect value.	SPT-36
Perform a stand-alone mobile device internal memory acquisition and review the status flags for text messages present on the SIM.	SPT-37
Acquire SIM memory and review hash values for vendor supported data objects.	SPT-39
Acquire mobile device internal memory and review data containing GPS longitude and latitude coordinates.	SPT-40

3 Results by Test Assertion

A test assertion is a verifiable statement about a single condition after an action is performed by the tool under test. A test case usually checks a group of assertions after the action of a single execution of the tool under test. Test assertions are defined and linked to test cases in *Smart Phone Tool Test Assertions and Test Plan Version 1.0*.

Tables 3a–3f summarize the test results by assertion. The column labeled **Assertions Tested** describes the text of each assertion. The column labeled **Tests** gives the number of test cases that use the given assertion. The column labeled **Anomaly** gives the section number in this report where any anomalies are discussed.

Table 3a: Assertions Tested (iPhone4 GSM)

Assertions Tested	Tests	Anomaly
SPT-CA-01 If a cellular forensic tool provides support for connectivity of the target device, then the tool shall successfully recognize the target device via all vendor supported interfaces (e.g., cable, Bluetooth, IrDA).	1	
SPT-CA-02 If a cellular forensic tool attempts to connect to a nonsupported device, then the tool shall notify the user that the device is not supported.	1	
SPT-CA-03 If connectivity between the mobile device and cellular forensic tool is disrupted, then the tool shall notify the user that connectivity has been disrupted.	1	
SPT-CA-04 If a cellular forensic tool completes acquisition of the target device without error, then the tool shall have the ability to present acquired data objects in a useable format via either a preview pane or generated report.	2	
SPT-CA-05 If a cellular forensic tool completes acquisition of the target	1	3.2

Assertions Tested	Tests	Anomaly
device without error, then subscriber related information shall be presented in a useable format.		
SPT-CA-06 If a cellular forensic tool completes acquisition of the target device without error, then equipment-related information shall be presented in a useable format.	1	
SPT-CA-07 If a cellular forensic tool completes acquisition of the target device without error, then address book entries shall be presented in a useable format.	1	
SPT-CA-08 If a cellular forensic tool completes acquisition of the target device without error, then maximum length address book entries shall be presented in a useable format.	1	
SPT-CA-09 If a cellular forensic tool completes acquisition of the target device without error, then address book entries containing special characters shall be presented in a useable format.	1	
SPT-CA-10 If a cellular forensic tool completes acquisition of the target device without error, then address book entries containing blank names shall be presented in a useable format.	1	
SPT-CA-11 If a cellular forensic tool completes acquisition of the target device without error, then email addresses associated with address book entries shall be presented in a useable format.	1	
SPT-CA-12 If a cellular forensic tool completes acquisition of the target device without error, then graphics associated with address book entries shall be presented in a useable format.	1	3.3
SPT-CA-13 If a cellular forensic tool completes acquisition of the target device without error, then datebook, calendar, note entries shall be presented in a useable format.	1	
SPT-CA-14 If a cellular forensic tool completes acquisition of the target device without error, then maximum length datebook, calendar, note entries shall be presented in a useable format.	1	
SPT-CA-15 If a cellular forensic tool completes acquisition of the target device without error, then call logs (incoming/outgoing/missed) shall be presented in a useable format.	1	3.4
SPT-CA-16 If a cellular forensic tool completes acquisition of the target device without error, then the corresponding date/time stamps and the duration of the call for call logs shall be presented in a useable format.	1	
SPT-CA-17 If a cellular forensic tool completes acquisition of the target device without error, then ASCII text messages (i.e., SMS, EMS) shall be presented in a useable format.	1	
SPT-CA-18 If a cellular forensic tool completes acquisition of the target device without error, then the corresponding date/time stamps for text messages shall be presented in a useable format.	1	
SPT-CA-19 If a cellular forensic tool completes acquisition of the target device without error, then the corresponding status (i.e., read, unread) for text messages shall be presented in a useable format.	1	3.5
SPT-CA-20 If a cellular forensic tool completes acquisition of the target	1	

Assertions Tested	Tests	Anomaly
device without error, then the corresponding sender / recipient phone numbers for text messages shall be presented in a useable format.		
SPT-CA-21 If a cellular forensic tool completes acquisition of the target device without error, then MMS messages and associated audio shall be presented in a useable format.	1	3.6
SPT-CA-22 If a cellular forensic tool completes acquisition of the target device without error, then MMS messages and associated graphic files shall be presented in a useable format.	1	
SPT-CA-23 If a cellular forensic tool completes acquisition of the target device without error, then MMS messages and associated video shall be presented in a useable format.	1	
SPT-CA-24 If a cellular forensic tool completes acquisition of the target device without error, then stand-alone audio files shall be presented in a useable format via either an internal application or suggested third-party application.	1	3.7
SPT-CA-25 If a cellular forensic tool completes acquisition of the target device without error, then stand-alone graphic files shall be presented in a useable format via either an internal application or suggested third-party application.	1	
SPT-CA-26 If a cellular forensic tool completes acquisition of the target device without error, then stand-alone video files shall be presented in a useable format via either an internal application or suggested third-party application.	1	3.7
SPT-CA-28 If a cellular forensic tool completes acquisition of the target device without error, then Internet-related data (i.e., bookmarks, visited sites) cached to the device shall be acquired and presented in a useable format.	1	
SPT-CA-29 If a cellular forensic tool provides the user with an "Acquire All" device data objects acquisition option, then the tool shall complete the acquisition of all data objects without error.	2	
SPT-CA-30 If a cellular forensic tool provides the user with a "Select All" individual device data objects, then the tool shall complete the acquisition of all individually selected data objects without error.	2	
SPT-CA-31 If a cellular forensic tool provides the user with the ability to "Select Individual" device data objects for acquisition, then the tool shall acquire each exclusive data object without error.	2	
SPT-CA-32 If a cellular forensic tool completes two consecutive logical acquisitions of the target device without error, then the payload (data objects) on the mobile device shall remain consistent.	1	
SPT-AO-01 If a cellular forensic tool provides support for connectivity of the target SIM, then the tool shall successfully recognize the target SIM via all tool-supported interfaces (e.g., PC/SC reader, proprietary reader, mart phone itself).	2	
SPT-AO-02 If a cellular forensic tool attempts to connect to a nonsupported SIM, then the tool shall notify the user that the SIM is not	1	

Assertions Tested	Tests	Anomaly
supported.		
SPT-AO-03 If a cellular forensic tool loses connectivity with the SIM reader, then the tool shall notify the user that connectivity has been disrupted.	1	
SPT-AO-04 If a cellular forensic tool completes acquisition of the target SIM without error, then the SPN shall be presented in a useable format.	1	
SPT-AO-05 If a cellular forensic tool completes acquisition of the target SIM without error, then the ICCID shall be presented in a useable format.	1	
SPT-AO-06 If a cellular forensic tool completes acquisition of the target SIM without error, then the IMSI shall be presented in a useable format.	1	
SPT-AO-07 If a cellular forensic tool completes acquisition of the target SIM without error, then the MSISDN shall be presented in a useable format.	1	
SPT-AO-08 If a cellular forensic tool completes acquisition of the target SIM without error, then ASCII Abbreviated Dialing Numbers (ADN) shall be presented in a useable format.	1	
SPT-AO-09 If a cellular forensic tool completes acquisition of the target SIM without error, then maximum length ADNs shall be presented in a useable format.	1	
SPT-AO-10 If a cellular forensic tool completes acquisition of the SIM without error, then ADNs containing special characters shall be presented in a useable format.	1	
SPT-AO-11 If a cellular forensic tool completes acquisition of the SIM without error, then ADNs containing blank names shall be presented in a useable format.	1	
SPT-AO-12 If a cellular forensic tool completes acquisition of the target SIM without error, then Last Numbers Dialed (LND) shall be presented in a useable format.	1	
SPT-AO-13 If a cellular forensic tool completes acquisition of the target SIM without error, then the corresponding date/time stamps for LNDs shall be presented in a useable format.	1	
SPT-AO-14 If a cellular forensic tool completes acquisition of the target SIM without error, then ASCII SMS text messages shall be presented in a useable format.	1	
SPT-AO-15 If a cellular forensic tool completes acquisition of the target SIM without error, then ASCII EMS text messages shall be presented in a useable format.	1	
SPT-AO-16 If a cellular forensic tool completes acquisition of the target SIM without error, then the corresponding date/time stamps for all text messages shall be presented in a useable format.	1	
SPT-AO-17 If a cellular forensic tool completes acquisition of the target SIM without error, then the corresponding status (i.e., read, unread) for text messages shall be presented in a useable format.	1	
SPT-AO-18 If a cellular forensic tool completes acquisition of the target	1	

Assertions Tested	Tests	Anomaly
SIM without error, then the corresponding sender / recipient phone numbers for text messages shall be presented in a useable format.		
SPT-AO-19 If the cellular forensic tool completes acquisition of the target SIM without error, then deleted text messages that have not been overwritten shall be presented in a useable format.	1	
SPT-AO-20 If a cellular forensic tool completes acquisition of the target SIM without error, then location-related data (i.e., LOCI) shall be presented in a useable format.	1	
SPT-AO-21 If a cellular forensic tool completes acquisition of the target SIM without error, then location-related data (i.e., GRPSLOCI) shall be presented in a useable format.	1	
SPT-AO-22 If a cellular forensic tool provides the user with an "Acquire All" SIM data objects acquisition option, then the tool shall complete the acquisition of all data objects without error.	1	
SPT-AO-23 If a cellular forensic tool provides the user with an "Select All" individual SIM data objects, then the tool shall complete the acquisition of all individually selected data objects without error.	1	
SPT-AO-24 If a cellular forensic tool provides the user with the ability to "Select Individual" SIM data objects for acquisition, then the tool shall acquire each exclusive data object without error.	1	
SPT-AO-25 If a cellular forensic tool completes acquisition of the SIM without error, then the tool shall present the acquired data in a useable format via supported generated report formats.	2	
SPT-AO-26 If a cellular forensic tool completes acquisition of the SIM without error, then the tool shall present the acquired data in a useable format in a preview pane view.	2	
SPT-AO-27 If the case file or individual data objects are modified via third-party means, then the tool shall provide protection mechanisms disallowing or reporting data modification.	2	
SPT-AO-28 If the SIM is password-protected, then the cellular forensic tool shall provide the examiner with the opportunity to input the PIN before acquisition.	1	
SPT-AO-29 If a cellular forensic tool provides the examiner with the remaining number of authentication attempts, then the application should provide an accurate count of the remaining PIN attempts.	1	
SPT-AO-30 If a cellular forensic tool provides the examiner with the remaining number of PUK attempts, then the application should provide an accurate count of the remaining PUK attempts.	1	
SPT-AO-40 If the cellular forensic tool supports display of non-ASCII characters, then the application should present ADNs in their native format.	2	
SPT-AO-41 If the cellular forensic tool supports proper display of non-ASCII characters, then the application should present text messages in their native format.	2	
SPT-AO-43 If the cellular forensic tool supports hashing for individual	2	

Assertions Tested	Tests	Anomaly
data objects, then the tool shall present the user with a hash value for each supported data object.		

Table 3b: Assertions Tested: (BlackBerry Torch)

Assertions Tested	Tests	Anomaly
SPT-CA-01 If a cellular forensic tool provides support for connectivity of the target device, then the tool shall successfully recognize the target device via all vendor supported interfaces (e.g., cable, Bluetooth, IrDA).	1	
SPT-CA-02 If a cellular forensic tool attempts to connect to a nonsupported device, then the tool shall notify the user that the device is not supported.	1	
SPT-CA-03 If connectivity between the mobile device and cellular forensic tool is disrupted, then the tool shall notify the user that connectivity has been disrupted.	1	
SPT-CA-04 If a cellular forensic tool completes acquisition of the target device without error, then the tool shall have the ability to present acquired data objects in a useable format via either a preview pane or generated report.	2	
SPT-CA-05 If a cellular forensic tool completes acquisition of the target device without error, then subscriber related information shall be presented in a useable format.	1	
SPT-CA-06 If a cellular forensic tool completes acquisition of the target device without error, then equipment-related information shall be presented in a useable format.	1	
SPT-CA-07 If a cellular forensic tool completes acquisition of the target device without error, then address book entries shall be presented in a useable format.	1	
SPT-CA-08 If a cellular forensic tool completes acquisition of the target device without error, then maximum length address book entries shall be presented in a useable format.	1	
SPT-CA-09 If a cellular forensic tool completes acquisition of the target device without error, then address book entries containing special characters shall be presented in a useable format.	1	
SPT-CA-10 If a cellular forensic tool completes acquisition of the target device without error, then address book entries containing blank names shall be presented in a useable format.	1	
SPT-CA-11 If a cellular forensic tool completes acquisition of the target device without error, then email addresses associated with address book entries shall be presented in a useable format.	1	
SPT-CA-12 If a cellular forensic tool completes acquisition of the target device without error, then graphics associated with address book entries shall be presented in a useable format.	1	3.3
SPT-CA-13 If a cellular forensic tool completes acquisition of the target device without error, then datebook, calendar, note entries shall be presented in a useable format.	1	
SPT-CA-14 If a cellular forensic tool completes acquisition of the target	1	

Assertions Tested	Tests	Anomaly
device without error, then maximum length datebook, calendar, note entries shall be presented in a useable format.		
SPT-CA-15 If a cellular forensic tool completes acquisition of the target device without error, then call logs (incoming/outgoing/missed) shall be presented in a useable format.	1	
SPT-CA-16 If a cellular forensic tool completes acquisition of the target device without error, then the corresponding date/time stamps and the duration of the call for call logs shall be presented in a useable format.	1	
SPT-CA-17 If a cellular forensic tool completes acquisition of the target device without error, then ASCII text messages (i.e., SMS, EMS) shall be presented in a useable format.	1	
SPT-CA-18 If a cellular forensic tool completes acquisition of the target device without error, then the corresponding date/time stamps for text messages shall be presented in a useable format.	1	
SPT-CA-19 If a cellular forensic tool completes acquisition of the target device without error, then the corresponding status (i.e., read, unread) for text messages shall be presented in a useable format.	1	
SPT-CA-20 If a cellular forensic tool completes acquisition of the target device without error, then the corresponding sender / recipient phone numbers for text messages shall be presented in a useable format.	1	
SPT-CA-21 If a cellular forensic tool completes acquisition of the target device without error, then MMS messages and associated audio shall be presented in a useable format.	1	3.6
SPT-CA-22 If a cellular forensic tool completes acquisition of the target device without error, then MMS messages and associated graphic files shall be presented in a useable format.	1	3.6
SPT-CA-23 If a cellular forensic tool completes acquisition of the target device without error, then MMS messages and associated video shall be presented in a useable format.	1	3.6
SPT-CA-24 If a cellular forensic tool completes acquisition of the target device without error, then stand-alone audio files shall be presented in a useable format via either an internal application or suggested third-party application.	1	3.7
SPT-CA-25 If a cellular forensic tool completes acquisition of the target device without error, then stand-alone graphic files shall be presented in a useable format via either an internal application or suggested third-party application.	1	3.7
SPT-CA-26 If a cellular forensic tool completes acquisition of the target device without error, then stand-alone video files shall be presented in a useable format via either an internal application or suggested third-party application.	1	3.7
SPT-CA-28 If a cellular forensic tool completes acquisition of the target device without error, then Internet-related data (i.e., bookmarks, visited sites) cached to the device shall be acquired and presented in a useable format.	1	

Assertions Tested	Tests	Anomaly
SPT-CA-29 If a cellular forensic tool provides the user with an "Acquire All" device data objects acquisition option, then the tool shall complete the acquisition of all data objects without error.	2	
SPT-CA-30 If a cellular forensic tool provides the user with a "Select All" individual device data objects, then the tool shall complete the acquisition of all individually selected data objects without error.	2	
SPT-CA-31 If a cellular forensic tool provides the user with the ability to "Select Individual" device data objects for acquisition, then the tool shall acquire each exclusive data object without error.	2	
SPT-CA-32 If a cellular forensic tool completes two consecutive logical acquisitions of the target device without error, then the payload (data objects) on the mobile device shall remain consistent.	1	
SPT-AO-01 If a cellular forensic tool provides support for connectivity of the target SIM, then the tool shall successfully recognize the target SIM via all tool-supported interfaces (e.g., PC/SC reader, proprietary reader, Smart Phone itself).	2	
SPT-AO-02 If a cellular forensic tool attempts to connect to a nonsupported SIM, then the tool shall notify the user that the SIM is not supported.	1	
SPT-AO-03 If a cellular forensic tool loses connectivity with the SIM reader, then the tool shall notify the user that connectivity has been disrupted.	1	
SPT-AO-08 If a cellular forensic tool completes acquisition of the target SIM without error, then ASCII Abbreviated Dialing Numbers (ADN) shall be presented in a useable format.	1	
SPT-AO-09 If a cellular forensic tool completes acquisition of the target SIM without error, then maximum length ADNs shall be presented in a useable format.	1	
SPT-AO-10 If a cellular forensic tool completes acquisition of the SIM without error, then ADNs containing special characters shall be presented in a useable format.	1	
SPT-AO-11 If a cellular forensic tool completes acquisition of the SIM without error, then ADNs containing blank names shall be presented in a useable format.	1	
SPT-AO-12 If a cellular forensic tool completes acquisition of the target SIM without error, then Last Numbers Dialed (LND) shall be presented in a useable format.	1	
SPT-AO-13 If a cellular forensic tool completes acquisition of the target SIM without error, then the corresponding date/time stamps for LNDs shall be presented in a useable format.	1	
SPT-AO-14 If a cellular forensic tool completes acquisition of the target SIM without error, then ASCII SMS text messages shall be presented in a useable format.	1	
SPT-AO-15 If a cellular forensic tool completes acquisition of the target SIM without error, then ASCII EMS text messages shall be presented in	1	

Assertions Tested	Tests	Anomaly
a useable format.		
SPT-AO-16 If a cellular forensic tool completes acquisition of the target SIM without error, then the corresponding date/time stamps for all text messages shall be presented in a useable format.	1	
SPT-AO-17 If a cellular forensic tool completes acquisition of the target SIM without error, then the corresponding status (i.e., read, unread) for text messages shall be presented in a useable format.	1	
SPT-AO-18 If a cellular forensic tool completes acquisition of the target SIM without error, then the corresponding sender / recipient phone numbers for text messages shall be presented in a useable format.	1	
SPT-AO-19 If the cellular forensic tool completes acquisition of the target SIM without error, then deleted text messages that have not been overwritten shall be presented in a useable format.	1	
SPT-AO-20 If a cellular forensic tool completes acquisition of the target SIM without error, then location-related data (i.e., LOCI) shall be presented in a useable format.	1	
SPT-AO-21 If a cellular forensic tool completes acquisition of the target SIM without error, then location-related data (i.e., GRPSLOCI) shall be presented in a useable format.	1	
SPT-AO-22 If a cellular forensic tool provides the user with an "Acquire All" SIM data objects acquisition option, then the tool shall complete the acquisition of all data objects without error.	1	
SPT-AO-23 If a cellular forensic tool provides the user with an "Select All" individual SIM data objects, then the tool shall complete the acquisition of all individually selected data objects without error.	1	
SPT-AO-24 If a cellular forensic tool provides the user with the ability to "Select Individual" SIM data objects for acquisition, then the tool shall acquire each exclusive data object without error.	1	
SPT-AO-25 If a cellular forensic tool completes acquisition of the SIM without error, then the tool shall present the acquired data in a useable format via supported generated report formats.	2	
SPT-AO-26 If a cellular forensic tool completes acquisition of the SIM without error, then the tool shall present the acquired data in a useable format in a preview pane view.	2	
SPT-AO-27 If the case file or individual data objects are modified via third-party means, then the tool shall provide protection mechanisms disallowing or reporting data modification.	2	
SPT-AO-28 If the SIM is password-protected, then the cellular forensic tool shall provide the examiner with the opportunity to input the PIN before acquisition.	1	
SPT-AO-29 If a cellular forensic tool provides the examiner with the remaining number of authentication attempts, then the application should provide an accurate count of the remaining PIN attempts.	1	
SPT-AO-30 If a cellular forensic tool provides the examiner with the remaining number of PUK attempts, then the application should provide	1	

Assertions Tested	Tests	Anomaly
an accurate count of the remaining PUK attempts.		
SPT-AO-40 If the cellular forensic tool supports display of non-ASCII characters, then the application should present ADNs in their native format.	2	3.10
SPT-AO-41 If the cellular forensic tool supports proper display of non-ASCII characters, then the application should present text messages in their native format.	2	3.10
SPT-AO-43 If the cellular forensic tool supports hashing for individual data objects, then the tool shall present the user with a hash value for each supported data object.	2	

Table 3c: Assertions Tested: (Nokia 6350)

Assertions Tested	Tests	Anomaly
SPT-CA-01 If a cellular forensic tool provides support for connectivity of the target device, then the tool shall successfully recognize the target device via all vendor supported interfaces (e.g., cable, Bluetooth, IrDA).	1	3.1
SPT-CA-04 If a cellular forensic tool completes acquisition of the target device without error, then the tool shall have the ability to present acquired data objects in a useable format via either a preview pane or generated report.	1	
SPT-CA-29 If a cellular forensic tool provides the user with an "Acquire All" device data objects acquisition option, then the tool shall complete the acquisition of all data objects without error.	1	
SPT-CA-30 If a cellular forensic tool provides the user with a "Select All" individual device data objects, then the tool shall complete the acquisition of all individually selected data objects without error.	1	
SPT-CA-31 If a cellular forensic tool provides the user with the ability to "Select Individual" device data objects for acquisition, then the tool shall acquire each exclusive data object without error.	1	
SPT-CA-32 If a cellular forensic tool completes two consecutive logical acquisitions of the target device without error, then the payload (data objects) on the mobile device shall remain consistent.	1	
SPT-AO-01 If a cellular forensic tool provides support for connectivity of the target SIM, then the tool shall successfully recognize the target SIM via all tool-supported interfaces (e.g., PC/SC reader, proprietary reader, Smart Phone itself).	2	
SPT-AO-02 If a cellular forensic tool attempts to connect to a nonsupported SIM, then the tool shall notify the user that the SIM is not supported.	1	
SPT-AO-03 If a cellular forensic tool loses connectivity with the SIM reader, then the tool shall notify the user that connectivity has been disrupted.	1	
SPT-AO-04 If a cellular forensic tool completes acquisition of the target SIM without error, then the SPN shall be presented in a useable format.	1	
SPT-AO-05 If a cellular forensic tool completes acquisition of the target SIM without error, then the ICCID shall be presented in a useable	1	

Assertions Tested	Tests	Anomaly
format.		
SPT-AO-06 If a cellular forensic tool completes acquisition of the target SIM without error, then the IMSI shall be presented in a useable format.	1	
SPT-AO-07 If a cellular forensic tool completes acquisition of the target SIM without error, then the MSISDN shall be presented in a useable format.	1	
SPT-AO-08 If a cellular forensic tool completes acquisition of the target SIM without error, then ASCII Abbreviated Dialing Numbers (ADN) shall be presented in a useable format.	1	
SPT-AO-09 If a cellular forensic tool completes acquisition of the target SIM without error, then maximum length ADNs shall be presented in a useable format.	1	
SPT-AO-10 If a cellular forensic tool completes acquisition of the SIM without error, then ADNs containing special characters shall be presented in a useable format.	1	
SPT-AO-11 If a cellular forensic tool completes acquisition of the SIM without error, then ADNs containing blank names shall be presented in a useable format.	1	
SPT-AO-12 If a cellular forensic tool completes acquisition of the target SIM without error, then Last Numbers Dialed (LND) shall be presented in a useable format.	1	
SPT-AO-13 If a cellular forensic tool completes acquisition of the target SIM without error, then the corresponding date/time stamps for LNDs shall be presented in a useable format.	1	
SPT-AO-14 If a cellular forensic tool completes acquisition of the target SIM without error, then ASCII SMS text messages shall be presented in a useable format.	1	
SPT-AO-15 If a cellular forensic tool completes acquisition of the target SIM without error, then ASCII EMS text messages shall be presented in a useable format.	1	
SPT-AO-16 If a cellular forensic tool completes acquisition of the target SIM without error, then the corresponding date/time stamps for all text messages shall be presented in a useable format.	1	
SPT-AO-17 If a cellular forensic tool completes acquisition of the target SIM without error, then the corresponding status (i.e., read, unread) for text messages shall be presented in a useable format.	1	
SPT-AO-18 If a cellular forensic tool completes acquisition of the target SIM without error, then the corresponding sender / recipient phone numbers for text messages shall be presented in a useable format.	1	
SPT-AO-19 If the cellular forensic tool completes acquisition of the target SIM without error, then deleted text messages that have not been overwritten shall be presented in a useable format.	1	
SPT-AO-20 If a cellular forensic tool completes acquisition of the target SIM without error, then location-related data (i.e., LOCI) shall be presented in a useable format.	1	

Assertions Tested	Tests	Anomaly
SPT-AO-21 If a cellular forensic tool completes acquisition of the target SIM without error, then location-related data (i.e., GRPSLOCI) shall be presented in a useable format.	1	
SPT-AO-22 If a cellular forensic tool provides the user with an "Acquire All" SIM data objects acquisition option, then the tool shall complete the acquisition of all data objects without error.	1	
SPT-AO-23 If a cellular forensic tool provides the user with an "Select All" individual SIM data objects, then the tool shall complete the acquisition of all individually selected data objects without error.	1	
SPT-AO-24 If a cellular forensic tool provides the user with the ability to "Select Individual" SIM data objects for acquisition, then the tool shall acquire each exclusive data object without error.	1	
SPT-AO-25 If a cellular forensic tool completes acquisition of the SIM without error, then the tool shall present the acquired data in a useable format via supported generated report formats.	1	
SPT-AO-26 If a cellular forensic tool completes acquisition of the SIM without error, then the tool shall present the acquired data in a useable format in a preview pane view.	1	
SPT-AO-27 If the case file or individual data objects are modified via third-party means, then the tool shall provide protection mechanisms disallowing or reporting data modification.	1	
SPT-AO-28 If the SIM is password-protected, then the cellular forensic tool shall provide the examiner with the opportunity to input the PIN before acquisition.	1	
SPT-AO-29 If a cellular forensic tool provides the examiner with the remaining number of authentication attempts, then the application should provide an accurate count of the remaining PIN attempts.	1	
SPT-AO-30 If a cellular forensic tool provides the examiner with the remaining number of PUK attempts, then the application should provide an accurate count of the remaining PUK attempts.	1	
SPT-AO-40 If the cellular forensic tool supports display of non-ASCII characters, then the application should present ADNs in their native format.	1	
SPT-AO-41 If the cellular forensic tool supports proper display of non-ASCII characters, then the application should present text messages in their native format.	1	
SPT-AO-43 If the cellular forensic tool supports hashing for individual data objects, then the tool shall present the user with a hash value for each supported data object.	1	

Table 3d: Assertions Tested: (iPhone4 CDMA)

Assertions Tested	Tests	Anomaly
SPT-CA-01 If a cellular forensic tool provides support for connectivity of the target device, then the tool shall successfully recognize the target device via all vendor supported interfaces (e.g., cable, Bluetooth, IrDA).	1	
SPT-CA-02 If a cellular forensic tool attempts to connect to a	1	

Assertions Tested	Tests	Anomaly
nonsupported device, then the tool shall notify the user that the device is not supported.		
SPT-CA-03 If connectivity between the mobile device and cellular forensic tool is disrupted, then the tool shall notify the user that connectivity has been disrupted.	1	
SPT-CA-04 If a cellular forensic tool completes acquisition of the target device without error, then the tool shall have the ability to present acquired data objects in a useable format via either a preview pane or generated report.	2	
SPT-CA-05 If a cellular forensic tool completes acquisition of the target device without error, then subscriber related information shall be presented in a useable format.	1	3.2
SPT-CA-06 If a cellular forensic tool completes acquisition of the target device without error, then equipment-related information shall be presented in a useable format.	1	3.2
SPT-CA-07 If a cellular forensic tool completes acquisition of the target device without error, then address book entries shall be presented in a useable format.	1	
SPT-CA-08 If a cellular forensic tool completes acquisition of the target device without error, then maximum length address book entries shall be presented in a useable format.	1	
SPT-CA-09 If a cellular forensic tool completes acquisition of the target device without error, then address book entries containing special characters shall be presented in a useable format.	1	
SPT-CA-10 If a cellular forensic tool completes acquisition of the target device without error, then address book entries containing blank names shall be presented in a useable format.	1	
SPT-CA-11 If a cellular forensic tool completes acquisition of the target device without error, then email addresses associated with address book entries shall be presented in a useable format.	1	
SPT-CA-12 If a cellular forensic tool completes acquisition of the target device without error, then graphics associated with address book entries shall be presented in a useable format.	1	3.3
SPT-CA-13 If a cellular forensic tool completes acquisition of the target device without error, then datebook, calendar, note entries shall be presented in a useable format.	1	
SPT-CA-14 If a cellular forensic tool completes acquisition of the target device without error, then maximum length datebook, calendar, note entries shall be presented in a useable format.	1	
SPT-CA-15 If a cellular forensic tool completes acquisition of the target device without error, then call logs (incoming/outgoing/missed) shall be presented in a useable format.	1	3.4
SPT-CA-16 If a cellular forensic tool completes acquisition of the target device without error, then the corresponding date/time stamps and the duration of the call for call logs shall be presented in a useable format.	1	

Assertions Tested	Tests	Anomaly
SPT-CA-17 If a cellular forensic tool completes acquisition of the target device without error, then ASCII text messages (i.e., SMS, EMS) shall be presented in a useable format.	1	
SPT-CA-18 If a cellular forensic tool completes acquisition of the target device without error, then the corresponding date/time stamps for text messages shall be presented in a useable format.	1	
SPT-CA-19 If a cellular forensic tool completes acquisition of the target device without error, then the corresponding status (i.e., read, unread) for text messages shall be presented in a useable format.	1	3.5
SPT-CA-20 If a cellular forensic tool completes acquisition of the target device without error, then the corresponding sender / recipient phone numbers for text messages shall be presented in a useable format.	1	
SPT-CA-21 If a cellular forensic tool completes acquisition of the target device without error, then MMS messages and associated audio shall be presented in a useable format.	1	3.6
SPT-CA-22 If a cellular forensic tool completes acquisition of the target device without error, then MMS messages and associated graphic files shall be presented in a useable format.	1	3.6
SPT-CA-23 If a cellular forensic tool completes acquisition of the target device without error, then MMS messages and associated video shall be presented in a useable format.	1	3.6
SPT-CA-24 If a cellular forensic tool completes acquisition of the target device without error, then stand-alone audio files shall be presented in a useable format via either an internal application or suggested third-party application.	1	3.7
SPT-CA-25 If a cellular forensic tool completes acquisition of the target device without error, then stand-alone graphic files shall be presented in a useable format via either an internal application or suggested third-party application.	1	
SPT-CA-26 If a cellular forensic tool completes acquisition of the target device without error, then stand-alone video files shall be presented in a useable format via either an internal application or suggested third-party application.	1	3.7
SPT-CA-28 If a cellular forensic tool completes acquisition of the target device without error, then Internet-related data (i.e., bookmarks, visited sites) cached to the device shall be acquired and presented in a useable format.	1	
SPT-CA-29 If a cellular forensic tool provides the user with an "Acquire All" device data objects acquisition option, then the tool shall complete the acquisition of all data objects without error.	2	
SPT-CA-30 If a cellular forensic tool provides the user with a "Select All" individual device data objects, then the tool shall complete the acquisition of all individually selected data objects without error.	2	
SPT-CA-31 If a cellular forensic tool provides the user with the ability to "Select Individual" device data objects for acquisition, then the tool	2	

Assertions Tested	Tests	Anomaly
shall acquire each exclusive data object without error.		
SPT-CA-32 If a cellular forensic tool completes two consecutive logical acquisitions of the target device without error, then the payload (data objects) on the mobile device shall remain consistent.	1	
SPT-AO-25 If a cellular forensic tool completes acquisition of the target device without error, then the tool shall present the acquired data in a useable format via supported generated report formats.	1	
SPT-AO-26 If a cellular forensic tool completes acquisition of the target device without error, then the tool shall present the acquired data in a useable format in a preview pane view.	1	
SPT-AO-27 If the case file or individual data objects are modified via third-party means, then the tool shall provide protection mechanisms disallowing or reporting data modification.	1	
SPT-AO-40 If the cellular forensic tool supports display of non-ASCII characters, then the application should present address book entries in their native format.	1	
SPT-AO-41 If the cellular forensic tool supports proper display of non-ASCII characters, then the application should present text messages in their native format.	1	
SPT-AO-43 If the cellular forensic tool supports hashing for individual data objects, then the tool shall present the user with a hash value for each supported data object.	1	

Table 3e: Assertions Tested: (HTC Thunderbolt)

Assertions Tested	Tests	Anomaly
SPT-CA-01 If a cellular forensic tool provides support for connectivity of the target device, then the tool shall successfully recognize the target device via all vendor supported interfaces (e.g., cable, Bluetooth, IrDA).	1	3.1
SPT-CA-02 If a cellular forensic tool attempts to connect to a nonsupported device, then the tool shall notify the user that the device is not supported.	1	
SPT-CA-03 If connectivity between the mobile device and cellular forensic tool is disrupted, then the tool shall notify the user that connectivity has been disrupted.	1	
SPT-CA-04 If a cellular forensic tool completes acquisition of the target device without error, then the tool shall have the ability to present acquired data objects in a useable format via either a preview pane or generated report.	2	
SPT-CA-05 If a cellular forensic tool completes acquisition of the target device without error, then subscriber related information shall be presented in a useable format.	1	
SPT-CA-06 If a cellular forensic tool completes acquisition of the target device without error, then equipment-related information shall be presented in a useable format.	1	
SPT-CA-07 If a cellular forensic tool completes acquisition of the target device without error, then address book entries shall be presented in a	1	

Assertions Tested	Tests	Anomaly
useable format.		
SPT-CA-08 If a cellular forensic tool completes acquisition of the target device without error, then maximum length address book entries shall be presented in a useable format.	1	
SPT-CA-09 If a cellular forensic tool completes acquisition of the target device without error, then address book entries containing special characters shall be presented in a useable format.	1	
SPT-CA-10 If a cellular forensic tool completes acquisition of the target device without error, then address book entries containing blank names shall be presented in a useable format.	1	
SPT-CA-11 If a cellular forensic tool completes acquisition of the target device without error, then email addresses associated with address book entries shall be presented in a useable format.	1	
SPT-CA-12 If a cellular forensic tool completes acquisition of the target device without error, then graphics associated with address book entries shall be presented in a useable format.	1	
SPT-CA-13 If a cellular forensic tool completes acquisition of the target device without error, then datebook, calendar, note entries shall be presented in a useable format.	1	3.3
SPT-CA-14 If a cellular forensic tool completes acquisition of the target device without error, then maximum length datebook, calendar, note entries shall be presented in a useable format.	1	
SPT-CA-15 If a cellular forensic tool completes acquisition of the target device without error, then call logs (incoming/outgoing/missed) shall be presented in a useable format.	1	
SPT-CA-16 If a cellular forensic tool completes acquisition of the target device without error, then the corresponding date/time stamps and the duration of the call for call logs shall be presented in a useable format.	1	
SPT-CA-17 If a cellular forensic tool completes acquisition of the target device without error, then ASCII text messages (i.e., SMS, EMS) shall be presented in a useable format.	1	
SPT-CA-18 If a cellular forensic tool completes acquisition of the target device without error, then the corresponding date/time stamps for text messages shall be presented in a useable format.	1	
SPT-CA-19 If a cellular forensic tool completes acquisition of the target device without error, then the corresponding status (i.e., read, unread) for text messages shall be presented in a useable format.	1	
SPT-CA-20 If a cellular forensic tool completes acquisition of the target device without error, then the corresponding sender / recipient phone numbers for text messages shall be presented in a useable format.	1	
SPT-CA-21 If a cellular forensic tool completes acquisition of the target device without error, then MMS messages and associated audio shall be presented in a useable format.	1	
SPT-CA-22 If a cellular forensic tool completes acquisition of the target device without error, then MMS messages and associated graphic files	1	

Assertions Tested	Tests	Anomaly
shall be presented in a useable format.		
SPT-CA-23 If a cellular forensic tool completes acquisition of the target device without error, then MMS messages and associated video shall be presented in a useable format.	1	
SPT-CA-24 If a cellular forensic tool completes acquisition of the target device without error, then stand-alone audio files shall be presented in a useable format via either an internal application or suggested third-party application.	1	3.7
SPT-CA-25 If a cellular forensic tool completes acquisition of the target device without error, then stand-alone graphic files shall be presented in a useable format via either an internal application or suggested third-party application.	1	3.7
SPT-CA-26 If a cellular forensic tool completes acquisition of the target device without error, then stand-alone video files shall be presented in a useable format via either an internal application or suggested third-party application.	1	3.7
SPT-CA-27 If a cellular forensic tool completes acquisition of the target device without error, then device specific application-related data shall be acquired and presented in a useable format via either an internal application or suggested third-party application.	1	3.8
SPT-CA-28 If a cellular forensic tool completes acquisition of the target device without error, then Internet-related data (i.e., bookmarks, visited sites) cached to the device shall be acquired and presented in a useable format.	1	
SPT-CA-29 If a cellular forensic tool provides the user with an "Acquire All" device data objects acquisition option, then the tool shall complete the acquisition of all data objects without error.	2	
SPT-CA-30 If a cellular forensic tool provides the user with a "Select All" individual device data objects, then the tool shall complete the acquisition of all individually selected data objects without error.	2	
SPT-CA-31 If a cellular forensic tool provides the user with the ability to "Select Individual" device data objects for acquisition, then the tool shall acquire each exclusive data object without error.	2	
SPT-CA-32 If a cellular forensic tool completes two consecutive logical acquisitions of the target device without error, then the payload (data objects) on the mobile device shall remain consistent.	1	
SPT-AO-25 If a cellular forensic tool completes acquisition of the target device without error, then the tool shall present the acquired data in a useable format via supported generated report formats.	1	
SPT-AO-26 If a cellular forensic tool completes acquisition of the target device without error, then the tool shall present the acquired data in a useable format in a preview pane view.	1	
SPT-AO-27 If the case file or individual data objects are modified via third-party means, then the tool shall provide protection mechanisms disallowing or reporting data modification.	1	

Assertions Tested	Tests	Anomaly
SPT-AO-40 If the cellular forensic tool supports display of non-ASCII characters, then the application should present address book entries in their native format.	1	
SPT-AO-41 If the cellular forensic tool supports proper display of non-ASCII characters, then the application should present text messages in their native format.	1	
SPT-AO-43 If the cellular forensic tool supports hashing for individual data objects, then the tool shall present the user with a hash value for each supported data object.	1	

Table 3f: Assertions Tested: (Palm Pre2)

Assertions Tested	Tests	Anomaly
SPT-CA-01 If a cellular forensic tool provides support for connectivity of the target device, then the tool shall successfully recognize the target device via all vendor supported interfaces (e.g., cable, Bluetooth, IrDA).	1	
SPT-CA-02 If a cellular forensic tool attempts to connect to a nonsupported device, then the tool shall notify the user that the device is not supported.	1	
SPT-CA-03 If connectivity between the mobile device and cellular forensic tool is disrupted, then the tool shall notify the user that connectivity has been disrupted.	1	
SPT-CA-04 If a cellular forensic tool completes acquisition of the target device without error, then the tool shall have the ability to present acquired data objects in a useable format via either a preview pane or generated report.	2	
SPT-CA-05 If a cellular forensic tool completes acquisition of the target device without error, then subscriber related information shall be presented in a useable format.	1	3.2
SPT-CA-06 If a cellular forensic tool completes acquisition of the target device without error, then equipment-related information shall be presented in a useable format.	1	3.2
SPT-CA-07 If a cellular forensic tool completes acquisition of the target device without error, then address book entries shall be presented in a useable format.	1	3.3
SPT-CA-08 If a cellular forensic tool completes acquisition of the target device without error, then maximum length address book entries shall be presented in a useable format.	1	
SPT-CA-09 If a cellular forensic tool completes acquisition of the target device without error, then address book entries containing special characters shall be presented in a useable format.	1	
SPT-CA-10 If a cellular forensic tool completes acquisition of the target device without error, then address book entries containing blank names shall be presented in a useable format.	1	
SPT-CA-11 If a cellular forensic tool completes acquisition of the target device without error, then email addresses associated with address book entries shall be presented in a useable format.	1	

Assertions Tested	Tests	Anomaly
SPT-CA-12 If a cellular forensic tool completes acquisition of the target device without error, then graphics associated with address book entries shall be presented in a useable format.	1	
SPT-CA-13 If a cellular forensic tool completes acquisition of the target device without error, then datebook, calendar, note entries shall be presented in a useable format.	1	3.3
SPT-CA-14 If a cellular forensic tool completes acquisition of the target device without error, then maximum length datebook, calendar, note entries shall be presented in a useable format.	1	
SPT-CA-15 If a cellular forensic tool completes acquisition of the target device without error, then call logs (incoming/outgoing/missed) shall be presented in a useable format.	1	3.4
SPT-CA-16 If a cellular forensic tool completes acquisition of the target device without error, then the corresponding date/time stamps and the duration of the call for call logs shall be presented in a useable format.	1	3.4
SPT-CA-17 If a cellular forensic tool completes acquisition of the target device without error, then ASCII text messages (i.e., SMS, EMS) shall be presented in a useable format.	1	3.5
SPT-CA-18 If a cellular forensic tool completes acquisition of the target device without error, then the corresponding date/time stamps for text messages shall be presented in a useable format.	1	
SPT-CA-19 If a cellular forensic tool completes acquisition of the target device without error, then the corresponding status (i.e., read, unread) for text messages shall be presented in a useable format.	1	
SPT-CA-20 If a cellular forensic tool completes acquisition of the target device without error, then the corresponding sender / recipient phone numbers for text messages shall be presented in a useable format.	1	
SPT-CA-21 If a cellular forensic tool completes acquisition of the target device without error, then MMS messages and associated audio shall be presented in a useable format.	1	3.6
SPT-CA-22 If a cellular forensic tool completes acquisition of the target device without error, then MMS messages and associated graphic files shall be presented in a useable format.	1	3.6
SPT-CA-23 If a cellular forensic tool completes acquisition of the target device without error, then MMS messages and associated video shall be presented in a useable format.	1	3.6
SPT-CA-24 If a cellular forensic tool completes acquisition of the target device without error, then stand-alone audio files shall be presented in a useable format via either an internal application or suggested third-party application.	1	3.7
SPT-CA-25 If a cellular forensic tool completes acquisition of the target device without error, then stand-alone graphic files shall be presented in a useable format via either an internal application or suggested third-party application.	1	3.7
SPT-CA-26 If a cellular forensic tool completes acquisition of the target	1	3.7

Assertions Tested	Tests	Anomaly
device without error, then stand-alone video files shall be presented in a useable format via either an internal application or suggested third-party application.		
SPT-CA-27 If a cellular forensic tool completes acquisition of the target device without error, then device specific application-related data shall be acquired and presented in a useable format via either an internal application or suggested third-party application.	1	3.8
SPT-CA-28 If a cellular forensic tool completes acquisition of the target device without error, then Internet-related data (i.e., bookmarks, visited sites) cached to the device shall be acquired and presented in a useable format.	1	3.9
SPT-CA-29 If a cellular forensic tool provides the user with an "Acquire All" device data objects acquisition option, then the tool shall complete the acquisition of all data objects without error.	2	
SPT-CA-30 If a cellular forensic tool provides the user with a "Select All" individual device data objects, then the tool shall complete the acquisition of all individually selected data objects without error.	2	
SPT-CA-31 If a cellular forensic tool provides the user with the ability to "Select Individual" device data objects for acquisition, then the tool shall acquire each exclusive data object without error.	2	
SPT-CA-32 If a cellular forensic tool completes two consecutive logical acquisitions of the target device without error, then the payload (data objects) on the mobile device shall remain consistent.	1	
SPT-AO-25 If a cellular forensic tool completes acquisition of the target device without error, then the tool shall present the acquired data in a useable format via supported generated report formats.	1	
SPT-AO-26 If a cellular forensic tool completes acquisition of the target device without error, then the tool shall present the acquired data in a useable format in a preview pane view.	1	
SPT-AO-27 If the case file or individual data objects are modified via third-party means, then the tool shall provide protection mechanisms disallowing or reporting data modification.	1	
SPT-AO-43 If the cellular forensic tool supports hashing for individual data objects, then the tool shall present the user with a hash value for each supported data object.	1	

Tables 4a–4f list the assertions that were not tested, usually due to the tool not supporting an optional feature.

Table 4a: Assertions Not Tested (iPhone4 GSM)

Assertions Not Tested
SPT-CA-27 If a cellular forensic tool completes acquisition of the target device without error, then device specific application-related data shall be acquired and presented in a useable format via either an internal application or suggested third-party application.

Assertions Not Tested
SPT-AO-31 If the cellular forensic tool supports a physical acquisition of the target device, then the tool shall complete the acquisition without error.
SPT-AO-32 If the cellular forensic tool supports the interpretation of address book entries present on the target device, then the tool shall report recoverable active and deleted data or address book data remnants in a useable format.
SPT-AO-33 If the cellular forensic tool supports the interpretation of calendar, tasks, or notes present on the target device, then the tool shall report recoverable active and deleted calendar, tasks, or note data remnants in a useable format.
SPT-AO-34 If the cellular forensic tool supports the interpretation of call logs present on the target device, then the tool shall report recoverable active and deleted call or call log data remnants in a useable format.
SPT-AO-35 If the cellular forensic tool supports the interpretation of SMS messages present on the target device, then the tool shall report recoverable active and deleted SMS messages or SMS message data remnants in a useable format.
SPT-AO-36 If the cellular forensic tool supports the interpretation of EMS messages present on the target device, then the tool shall report recoverable active and deleted EMS messages or EMS message data remnants in a useable format.
SPT-AO-37 If the cellular forensic tool supports the interpretation of audio files present on the target device, then the tool shall report recoverable active and deleted audio data or audio file data remnants in a useable format.
SPT-AO-38 If the cellular forensic tool supports the interpretation of graphic files present on the target device, then the tool shall report recoverable active and deleted graphic file data or graphic file data remnants in a useable format.
SPT-AO-39 If the cellular forensic tool supports the interpretation of video files present on the target device, then the tool shall report recoverable active and deleted video file data or video file data remnants in a useable format.
SPT-AO-42 If the cellular forensic tool supports stand-alone acquisition of internal memory with the SIM present, then the contents of the SIM shall not be modified during internal memory acquisition.
SPT-AO-44 If the cellular forensic tool supports acquisition of GPS data, then the tool shall present the user with the longitude and latitude coordinates for all GPS-related data in a useable format.

Table 4b: Assertions Not Tested (BlackBerry Torch)

Assertions Not Tested
SPT-CA-27 If a cellular forensic tool completes acquisition of the target device without error, then device specific application-related data shall be acquired and presented in a useable format via either an internal application or suggested third-party application.
SPT-AO-04 If a cellular forensic tool completes acquisition of the target SIM without error, then the SPN shall be presented in a useable format.
SPT-AO-05 If a cellular forensic tool completes acquisition of the target SIM without error, then the ICCID shall be presented in a useable format.
SPT-AO-06 If a cellular forensic tool completes acquisition of the target SIM without error, then the IMSI shall be presented in a useable format.
SPT-AO-07 If a cellular forensic tool completes acquisition of the target SIM without

Assertions Not Tested
error, then the MSISDN shall be presented in a useable format.
SPT-AO-31 If the cellular forensic tool supports a physical acquisition of the target device, then the tool shall complete the acquisition without error.
SPT-AO-32 If the cellular forensic tool supports the interpretation of address book entries present on the target device, then the tool shall report recoverable active and deleted data or address book data remnants in a useable format.
SPT-AO-33 If the cellular forensic tool supports the interpretation of calendar, tasks, or notes present on the target device, then the tool shall report recoverable active and deleted calendar, tasks, or note data remnants in a useable format.
SPT-AO-34 If the cellular forensic tool supports the interpretation of call logs present on the target device, then the tool shall report recoverable active and deleted call or call log data remnants in a useable format.
SPT-AO-35 If the cellular forensic tool supports the interpretation of SMS messages present on the target device, then the tool shall report recoverable active and deleted SMS messages or SMS message data remnants in a useable format.
SPT-AO-36 If the cellular forensic tool supports the interpretation of EMS messages present on the target device, then the tool shall report recoverable active and deleted EMS messages or EMS message data remnants in a useable format.
SPT-AO-37 If the cellular forensic tool supports the interpretation of audio files present on the target device, then the tool shall report recoverable active and deleted audio data or audio file data remnants in a useable format.
SPT-AO-38 If the cellular forensic tool supports the interpretation of graphic files present on the target device, then the tool shall report recoverable active and deleted graphic file data or graphic file data remnants in a useable format.
SPT-AO-39 If the cellular forensic tool supports the interpretation of video files present on the target device, then the tool shall report recoverable active and deleted video file data or video file data remnants in a useable format.
SPT-AO-42 If the cellular forensic tool supports stand-alone acquisition of internal memory with the SIM present, then the contents of the SIM shall not be modified during internal memory acquisition.
SPT-AO-44 If the cellular forensic tool supports acquisition of GPS data, then the tool shall present the user with the longitude and latitude coordinates for all GPS-related data in a useable format.

Table 4c: Assertions Not Tested (Nokia 6350)

Assertions Not Tested
SPT-CA-02 If a cellular forensic tool attempts to connect to a nonsupported device, then the tool shall notify the user that the device is not supported.
SPT-CA-03 If connectivity between the mobile device and cellular forensic tool is disrupted, then the tool shall notify the user that connectivity has been disrupted.
SPT-CA-05 If a cellular forensic tool completes acquisition of the target device without error, then subscriber related information shall be presented in a useable format.
SPT-CA-06 If a cellular forensic tool completes acquisition of the target device without error, then equipment-related information shall be presented in a useable format.
SPT-CA-07 If a cellular forensic tool completes acquisition of the target device without

Assertions Not Tested
error, then address book entries shall be presented in a useable format.
SPT-CA-08 If a cellular forensic tool completes acquisition of the target device without error, then maximum length address book entries shall be presented in a useable format.
SPT-CA-09 If a cellular forensic tool completes acquisition of the target device without error, then address book entries containing special characters shall be presented in a useable format.
SPT-CA-10 If a cellular forensic tool completes acquisition of the target device without error, then address book entries containing blank names shall be presented in a useable format.
SPT-CA-11 If a cellular forensic tool completes acquisition of the target device without error, then email addresses associated with address book entries shall be presented in a useable format.
SPT-CA-12 If a cellular forensic tool completes acquisition of the target device without error, then graphics associated with address book entries shall be presented in a useable format.
SPT-CA-13 If a cellular forensic tool completes acquisition of the target device without error, then datebook, calendar, note entries shall be presented in a useable format.
SPT-CA-14 If a cellular forensic tool completes acquisition of the target device without error, then maximum length datebook, calendar, note entries shall be presented in a useable format.
SPT-CA-15 If a cellular forensic tool completes acquisition of the target device without error, then call logs (incoming/outgoing/missed) shall be presented in a useable format.
SPT-CA-16 If a cellular forensic tool completes acquisition of the target device without error, then the corresponding date/time stamps and the duration of the call for call logs shall be presented in a useable format.
SPT-CA-17 If a cellular forensic tool completes acquisition of the target device without error, then ASCII text messages (i.e., SMS, EMS) shall be presented in a useable format.
SPT-CA-18 If a cellular forensic tool completes acquisition of the target device without error, then the corresponding date/time stamps for text messages shall be presented in a useable format.
SPT-CA-19 If a cellular forensic tool completes acquisition of the target device without error, then the corresponding status (i.e., read, unread) for text messages shall be presented in a useable format.
SPT-CA-20 If a cellular forensic tool completes acquisition of the target device without error, then the corresponding sender / recipient phone numbers for text messages shall be presented in a useable format.
SPT-CA-21 If a cellular forensic tool completes acquisition of the target device without error, then MMS messages and associated audio shall be presented in a useable format.
SPT-CA-22 If a cellular forensic tool completes acquisition of the target device without error, then MMS messages and associated graphic files shall be presented in a useable format.
SPT-CA-23 If a cellular forensic tool completes acquisition of the target device without error, then MMS messages and associated video shall be presented in a useable format.
SPT-CA-24 If a cellular forensic tool completes acquisition of the target device without error, then stand-alone audio files shall be presented in a useable format via either an

Assertions Not Tested
internal application or suggested third-party application.
SPT-CA-25 If a cellular forensic tool completes acquisition of the target device without error, then stand-alone graphic files shall be presented in a useable format via either an internal application or suggested third-party application.
SPT-CA-26 If a cellular forensic tool completes acquisition of the target device without error, then stand-alone video files shall be presented in a useable format via either an internal application or suggested third-party application.
SPT-CA-27 If a cellular forensic tool completes acquisition of the target device without error, then device specific application-related data shall be acquired and presented in a useable format via either an internal application or suggested third-party application.
SPT-CA-28 If a cellular forensic tool completes acquisition of the target device without error, then Internet-related data (i.e., bookmarks, visited sites) cached to the device shall be acquired and presented in a useable format.
SPT-AO-31 If the cellular forensic tool supports a physical acquisition of the target device, then the tool shall complete the acquisition without error.
SPT-AO-32 If the cellular forensic tool supports the interpretation of address book entries present on the target device, then the tool shall report recoverable active and deleted data or address book data remnants in a useable format.
SPT-AO-33 If the cellular forensic tool supports the interpretation of calendar, tasks, or notes present on the target device, then the tool shall report recoverable active and deleted calendar, tasks, or note data remnants in a useable format.
SPT-AO-34 If the cellular forensic tool supports the interpretation of call logs present on the target device, then the tool shall report recoverable active and deleted call or call log data remnants in a useable format.
SPT-AO-35 If the cellular forensic tool supports the interpretation of SMS messages present on the target device, then the tool shall report recoverable active and deleted SMS messages or SMS message data remnants in a useable format.
SPT-AO-36 If the cellular forensic tool supports the interpretation of EMS messages present on the target device, then the tool shall report recoverable active and deleted EMS messages or EMS message data remnants in a useable format.
SPT-AO-37 If the cellular forensic tool supports the interpretation of audio files present on the target device, then the tool shall report recoverable active and deleted audio data or audio file data remnants in a useable format.
SPT-AO-38 If the cellular forensic tool supports the interpretation of graphic files present on the target device, then the tool shall report recoverable active and deleted graphic file data or graphic file data remnants in a useable format.
SPT-AO-39 If the cellular forensic tool supports the interpretation of video files present on the target device, then the tool shall report recoverable active and deleted video file data or video file data remnants in a useable format.
SPT-AO-42 If the cellular forensic tool supports stand-alone acquisition of internal memory with the SIM present, then the contents of the SIM shall not be modified during internal memory acquisition.
SPT-AO-44 If the cellular forensic tool supports acquisition of GPS data, then the tool shall present the user with the longitude and latitude coordinates for all GPS-related data in a useable format.

Table 4d: Assertions Not Tested (iPhone4 CDMA)

Assertions Not Tested
SPT-CA-27 If a cellular forensic tool completes acquisition of the target device without error, then device specific application-related data shall be acquired and presented in a useable format via either an internal application or suggested third-party application.
SPT-AO-01 If a cellular forensic tool provides support for connectivity of the target SIM, then the tool shall successfully recognize the target SIM via all tool-supported interfaces (e.g., PC/SC reader, proprietary reader, Smart Phone itself).
SPT-AO-02 If a cellular forensic tool attempts to connect to a nonsupported SIM, then the tool shall notify the user that the SIM is not supported.
SPT-AO-03 If a cellular forensic tool loses connectivity with the SIM reader, then the tool shall notify the user that connectivity has been disrupted.
SPT-AO-04 If a cellular forensic tool completes acquisition of the target SIM without error, then the SPN shall be presented in a useable format.
SPT-AO-05 If a cellular forensic tool completes acquisition of the target SIM without error, then the ICCID shall be presented in a useable format.
SPT-AO-06 If a cellular forensic tool completes acquisition of the target SIM without error, then the IMSI shall be presented in a useable format.
SPT-AO-07 If a cellular forensic tool completes acquisition of the target SIM without error, then the MSISDN shall be presented in a useable format.
SPT-AO-08 If a cellular forensic tool completes acquisition of the target SIM without error, then ASCII Abbreviated Dialing Numbers (ADN) shall be presented in a useable format.
SPT-AO-09 If a cellular forensic tool completes acquisition of the target SIM without error, then maximum length ADNs shall be presented in a useable format.
SPT-AO-10 If a cellular forensic tool completes acquisition of the SIM without error, then ADNs containing special characters shall be presented in a useable format.
SPT-AO-11 If a cellular forensic tool completes acquisition of the SIM without error, then ADNs containing blank names shall be presented in a useable format.
SPT-AO-12 If a cellular forensic tool completes acquisition of the target SIM without error, then Last Numbers Dialed (LND) shall be presented in a useable format.
SPT-AO-13 If a cellular forensic tool completes acquisition of the target SIM without error, then the corresponding date/time stamps for LNDs shall be presented in a useable format.
SPT-AO-14 If a cellular forensic tool completes acquisition of the target SIM without error, then ASCII SMS text messages shall be presented in a useable format.
SPT-AO-15 If a cellular forensic tool completes acquisition of the target SIM without error, then ASCII EMS text messages shall be presented in a useable format.
SPT-AO-16 If a cellular forensic tool completes acquisition of the target SIM without error, then the corresponding date/time stamps for all text messages shall be presented in a useable format.
SPT-AO-17 If a cellular forensic tool completes acquisition of the target SIM without error, then the corresponding status (i.e., read, unread) for text messages shall be presented in a useable format.

Assertions Not Tested
SPT-AO-18 If a cellular forensic tool completes acquisition of the target SIM without error, then the corresponding sender / recipient phone numbers for text messages shall be presented in a useable format.
SPT-AO-19 If the cellular forensic tool completes acquisition of the target SIM without error, then deleted text messages that have not been overwritten shall be presented in a useable format.
SPT-AO-20 If a cellular forensic tool completes acquisition of the target SIM without error, then location-related data (i.e., LOCI) shall be presented in a useable format.
SPT-AO-21 If a cellular forensic tool completes acquisition of the target SIM without error, then location-related data (i.e., GRPSLOCI) shall be presented in a useable format.
SPT-AO-22 If a cellular forensic tool provides the user with an "Acquire All" SIM data objects acquisition option, then the tool shall complete the acquisition of all data objects without error.
SPT-AO-23 If a cellular forensic tool provides the user with a "Select All" individual SIM data objects, then the tool shall complete the acquisition of all individually selected data objects without error.
SPT-AO-24 If a cellular forensic tool provides the user with the ability to "Select Individual" SIM data objects for acquisition, then the tool shall acquire each exclusive data object without error.
SPT-AO-28 If the SIM is password-protected, then the cellular forensic tool shall provide the examiner with the opportunity to input the PIN before acquisition.
SPT-AO-29 If a cellular forensic tool provides the examiner with the remaining number of authentication attempts, then the application should provide an accurate count of the remaining PIN attempts.
SPT-AO-30 If a cellular forensic tool provides the examiner with the remaining number of PUK attempts, then the application should provide an accurate count of the remaining PUK attempts.
SPT-AO-31 If the cellular forensic tool supports a physical acquisition of the target device, then the tool shall complete the acquisition without error.
SPT-AO-32 If the cellular forensic tool supports the interpretation of address book entries present on the target device, then the tool shall report recoverable active and deleted data or address book data remnants in a useable format.
SPT-AO-33 If the cellular forensic tool supports the interpretation of calendar, tasks, or notes present on the target device, then the tool shall report recoverable active and deleted calendar, tasks, or note data remnants in a useable format.
SPT-AO-34 If the cellular forensic tool supports the interpretation of call logs present on the target device, then the tool shall report recoverable active and deleted call or call log data remnants in a useable format.
SPT-AO-35 If the cellular forensic tool supports the interpretation of SMS messages present on the target device, then the tool shall report recoverable active and deleted SMS messages or SMS message data remnants in a useable format.
SPT-AO-36 If the cellular forensic tool supports the interpretation of EMS messages present on the target device, then the tool shall report recoverable active and deleted EMS messages or EMS message data remnants in a useable format.
SPT-AO-37 If the cellular forensic tool supports the interpretation of audio files present

Assertions Not Tested
on the target device, then the tool shall report recoverable active and deleted audio data or audio file data remnants in a useable format.
SPT-AO-38 If the cellular forensic tool supports the interpretation of graphic files present on the target device, then the tool shall report recoverable active and deleted graphic file data or graphic file data remnants in a useable format.
SPT-AO-39 If the cellular forensic tool supports the interpretation of video files present on the target device, then the tool shall report recoverable active and deleted video file data or video file data remnants in a useable format.
SPT-AO-42 If the cellular forensic tool supports stand-alone acquisition of internal memory with the SIM present, then the contents of the SIM shall not be modified during internal memory acquisition.
SPT-AO-44 If the cellular forensic tool supports acquisition of GPS data, then the tool shall present the user with the longitude and latitude coordinates for all GPS-related data in a useable format.

Table 4e: Assertions Not Tested (HTC Thunderbolt)

Assertions Not Tested
SPT-AO-01 If a cellular forensic tool provides support for connectivity of the target SIM, then the tool shall successfully recognize the target SIM via all tool-supported interfaces (e.g., PC/SC reader, proprietary reader, Smart Phone itself).
SPT-AO-02 If a cellular forensic tool attempts to connect to a nonsupported SIM, then the tool shall notify the user that the SIM is not supported.
SPT-AO-03 If a cellular forensic tool loses connectivity with the SIM reader, then the tool shall notify the user that connectivity has been disrupted.
SPT-AO-04 If a cellular forensic tool completes acquisition of the target SIM without error, then the SPN shall be presented in a useable format.
SPT-AO-05 If a cellular forensic tool completes acquisition of the target SIM without error, then the ICCID shall be presented in a useable format.
SPT-AO-06 If a cellular forensic tool completes acquisition of the target SIM without error, then the IMSI shall be presented in a useable format.
SPT-AO-07 If a cellular forensic tool completes acquisition of the target SIM without error, then the MSISDN shall be presented in a useable format.
SPT-AO-08 If a cellular forensic tool completes acquisition of the target SIM without error, then ASCII Abbreviated Dialing Numbers (ADN) shall be presented in a useable format.
SPT-AO-09 If a cellular forensic tool completes acquisition of the target SIM without error, then maximum length ADNs shall be presented in a useable format.
SPT-AO-10 If a cellular forensic tool completes acquisition of the SIM without error, then ADNs containing special characters shall be presented in a useable format.
SPT-AO-11 If a cellular forensic tool completes acquisition of the SIM without error, then ADNs containing blank names shall be presented in a useable format.
SPT-AO-12 If a cellular forensic tool completes acquisition of the target SIM without error, then Last Numbers Dialed (LND) shall be presented in a useable format.
SPT-AO-13 If a cellular forensic tool completes acquisition of the target SIM without error, then the corresponding date/time stamps for LNDs shall be presented in a useable

Assertions Not Tested
format.
SPT-AO-14 If a cellular forensic tool completes acquisition of the target SIM without error, then ASCII SMS text messages shall be presented in a useable format.
SPT-AO-15 If a cellular forensic tool completes acquisition of the target SIM without error, then ASCII EMS text messages shall be presented in a useable format.
SPT-AO-16 If a cellular forensic tool completes acquisition of the target SIM without error, then the corresponding date/time stamps for all text messages shall be presented in a useable format.
SPT-AO-17 If a cellular forensic tool completes acquisition of the target SIM without error, then the corresponding status (i.e., read, unread) for text messages shall be presented in a useable format.
SPT-AO-18 If a cellular forensic tool completes acquisition of the target SIM without error, then the corresponding sender / recipient phone numbers for text messages shall be presented in a useable format.
SPT-AO-19 If the cellular forensic tool completes acquisition of the target SIM without error, then deleted text messages that have not been overwritten shall be presented in a useable format.
SPT-AO-20 If a cellular forensic tool completes acquisition of the target SIM without error, then location-related data (i.e., LOCI) shall be presented in a useable format.
SPT-AO-21 If a cellular forensic tool completes acquisition of the target SIM without error, then location-related data (i.e., GRPSLOCI) shall be presented in a useable format.
SPT-AO-22 If a cellular forensic tool provides the user with an "Acquire All" SIM data objects acquisition option, then the tool shall complete the acquisition of all data objects without error.
SPT-AO-23 If a cellular forensic tool provides the user with a "Select All" individual SIM data objects, then the tool shall complete the acquisition of all individually selected data objects without error.
SPT-AO-24 If a cellular forensic tool provides the user with the ability to "Select Individual" SIM data objects for acquisition, then the tool shall acquire each exclusive data object without error.
SPT-AO-28 If the SIM is password-protected, then the cellular forensic tool shall provide the examiner with the opportunity to input the PIN before acquisition.
SPT-AO-29 If a cellular forensic tool provides the examiner with the remaining number of authentication attempts, then the application should provide an accurate count of the remaining PIN attempts.
SPT-AO-30 If a cellular forensic tool provides the examiner with the remaining number of PUK attempts, then the application should provide an accurate count of the remaining PUK attempts.
SPT-AO-31 If the cellular forensic tool supports a physical acquisition of the target device, then the tool shall complete the acquisition without error.
SPT-AO-32 If the cellular forensic tool supports the interpretation of address book entries present on the target device, then the tool shall report recoverable active and deleted data or address book data remnants in a useable format.
SPT-AO-33 If the cellular forensic tool supports the interpretation of calendar, tasks, or notes present on the target device, then the tool shall report recoverable active and

Assertions Not Tested
deleted calendar, tasks, or note data remnants in a useable format.
SPT-AO-34 If the cellular forensic tool supports the interpretation of call logs present on the target device, then the tool shall report recoverable active and deleted call or call log data remnants in a useable format.
SPT-AO-35 If the cellular forensic tool supports the interpretation of SMS messages present on the target device, then the tool shall report recoverable active and deleted SMS messages or SMS message data remnants in a useable format.
SPT-AO-36 If the cellular forensic tool supports the interpretation of EMS messages present on the target device, then the tool shall report recoverable active and deleted EMS messages or EMS message data remnants in a useable format.
SPT-AO-37 If the cellular forensic tool supports the interpretation of audio files present on the target device, then the tool shall report recoverable active and deleted audio data or audio file data remnants in a useable format.
SPT-AO-38 If the cellular forensic tool supports the interpretation of graphic files present on the target device, then the tool shall report recoverable active and deleted graphic file data or graphic file data remnants in a useable format.
SPT-AO-39 If the cellular forensic tool supports the interpretation of video files present on the target device, then the tool shall report recoverable active and deleted video file data or video file data remnants in a useable format.
SPT-AO-42 If the cellular forensic tool supports stand-alone acquisition of internal memory with the SIM present, then the contents of the SIM shall not be modified during internal memory acquisition.
SPT-AO-44 If the cellular forensic tool supports acquisition of GPS data, then the tool shall present the user with the longitude and latitude coordinates for all GPS-related data in a useable format.

Table 4f: Assertions Not Tested (Palm Pre2)

Assertions Not Tested
SPT-AO-01 If a cellular forensic tool provides support for connectivity of the target SIM, then the tool shall successfully recognize the target SIM via all tool-supported interfaces (e.g., PC/SC reader, proprietary reader, Smart Phone itself).
SPT-AO-02 If a cellular forensic tool attempts to connect to a nonsupported SIM, then the tool shall notify the user that the SIM is not supported.
SPT-AO-03 If a cellular forensic tool loses connectivity with the SIM reader, then the tool shall notify the user that connectivity has been disrupted.
SPT-AO-04 If a cellular forensic tool completes acquisition of the target SIM without error, then the SPN shall be presented in a useable format.
SPT-AO-05 If a cellular forensic tool completes acquisition of the target SIM without error, then the ICCID shall be presented in a useable format.
SPT-AO-06 If a cellular forensic tool completes acquisition of the target SIM without error, then the IMSI shall be presented in a useable format.
SPT-AO-07 If a cellular forensic tool completes acquisition of the target SIM without error, then the MSISDN shall be presented in a useable format.
SPT-AO-08 If a cellular forensic tool completes acquisition of the target SIM without error, then ASCII Abbreviated Dialing Numbers (ADN) shall be presented in a useable

Assertions Not Tested
format.
SPT-AO-09 If a cellular forensic tool completes acquisition of the target SIM without error, then maximum length ADNs shall be presented in a useable format.
SPT-AO-10 If a cellular forensic tool completes acquisition of the SIM without error, then ADNs containing special characters shall be presented in a useable format.
SPT-AO-11 If a cellular forensic tool completes acquisition of the SIM without error, then ADNs containing blank names shall be presented in a useable format.
SPT-AO-12 If a cellular forensic tool completes acquisition of the target SIM without error, then Last Numbers Dialed (LND) shall be presented in a useable format.
SPT-AO-13 If a cellular forensic tool completes acquisition of the target SIM without error, then the corresponding date/time stamps for LNDs shall be presented in a useable format.
SPT-AO-14 If a cellular forensic tool completes acquisition of the target SIM without error, then ASCII SMS text messages shall be presented in a useable format.
SPT-AO-15 If a cellular forensic tool completes acquisition of the target SIM without error, then ASCII EMS text messages shall be presented in a useable format.
SPT-AO-16 If a cellular forensic tool completes acquisition of the target SIM without error, then the corresponding date/time stamps for all text messages shall be presented in a useable format.
SPT-AO-17 If a cellular forensic tool completes acquisition of the target SIM without error, then the corresponding status (i.e., read, unread) for text messages shall be presented in a useable format.
SPT-AO-18 If a cellular forensic tool completes acquisition of the target SIM without error, then the corresponding sender / recipient phone numbers for text messages shall be presented in a useable format.
SPT-AO-19 If the cellular forensic tool completes acquisition of the target SIM without error, then deleted text messages that have not been overwritten shall be presented in a useable format.
SPT-AO-20 If a cellular forensic tool completes acquisition of the target SIM without error, then location-related data (i.e., LOCI) shall be presented in a useable format.
SPT-AO-21 If a cellular forensic tool completes acquisition of the target SIM without error, then location-related data (i.e., GRPSLOCI) shall be presented in a useable format.
SPT-AO-22 If a cellular forensic tool provides the user with an "Acquire All" SIM data objects acquisition option, then the tool shall complete the acquisition of all data objects without error.
SPT-AO-23 If a cellular forensic tool provides the user with a "Select All" individual SIM data objects, then the tool shall complete the acquisition of all individually selected data objects without error.
SPT-AO-24 If a cellular forensic tool provides the user with the ability to "Select Individual" SIM data objects for acquisition, then the tool shall acquire each exclusive data object without error.
SPT-AO-28 If the SIM is password-protected, then the cellular forensic tool shall provide the examiner with the opportunity to input the PIN before acquisition.
SPT-AO-29 If a cellular forensic tool provides the examiner with the remaining number of authentication attempts, then the application should provide an accurate count of the

Assertions Not Tested
remaining PIN attempts.
SPT-AO-30 If a cellular forensic tool provides the examiner with the remaining number of PUK attempts, then the application should provide an accurate count of the remaining PUK attempts.
SPT-AO-31 If the cellular forensic tool supports a physical acquisition of the target device, then the tool shall complete the acquisition without error.
SPT-AO-32 If the cellular forensic tool supports the interpretation of address book entries present on the target device, then the tool shall report recoverable active and deleted data or address book data remnants in a useable format.
SPT-AO-33 If the cellular forensic tool supports the interpretation of calendar, tasks, or notes present on the target device, then the tool shall report recoverable active and deleted calendar, tasks, or note data remnants in a useable format.
SPT-AO-34 If the cellular forensic tool supports the interpretation of call logs present on the target device, then the tool shall report recoverable active and deleted call or call log data remnants in a useable format.
SPT-AO-35 If the cellular forensic tool supports the interpretation of SMS messages present on the target device, then the tool shall report recoverable active and deleted SMS messages or SMS message data remnants in a useable format.
SPT-AO-36 If the cellular forensic tool supports the interpretation of EMS messages present on the target device, then the tool shall report recoverable active and deleted EMS messages or EMS message data remnants in a useable format.
SPT-AO-37 If the cellular forensic tool supports the interpretation of audio files present on the target device, then the tool shall report recoverable active and deleted audio data or audio file data remnants in a useable format.
SPT-AO-38 If the cellular forensic tool supports the interpretation of graphic files present on the target device, then the tool shall report recoverable active and deleted graphic file data or graphic file data remnants in a useable format.
SPT-AO-39 If the cellular forensic tool supports the interpretation of video files present on the target device, then the tool shall report recoverable active and deleted video file data or video file data remnants in a useable format.
SPT-AO-40 If the cellular forensic tool supports display of non-ASCII characters, then the application should present ADNs in their native format.
SPT-AO-41 If the cellular forensic tool supports proper display of non-ASCII characters, then the application should present text messages in their native format.
SPT-AO-42 If the cellular forensic tool supports stand-alone acquisition of internal memory with the SIM present, then the contents of the SIM shall not be modified during internal memory acquisition.
SPT-AO-44 If the cellular forensic tool supports acquisition of GPS data, then the tool shall present the user with the longitude and latitude coordinates for all GPS-related data in a useable format.

The following sections provide detailed information for the anomalies from Tables 3a – 3f.

3.1 Device connectivity

For test case SPT-01, connectivity to the Nokia 6350 was not established using the supported interface. The following error was reported: "Acquisition process has failed – Result: Connection Error."

Acquisition of the HTC Thunderbolt ended in errors. The following error was reported: "Acquisition process has failed. Result – Connection broken." *Note: This anomaly was corrected with Device Seizure Version 5.0 build 4664.26841.*

3.2 Acquisition of subscriber- and equipment-related information

Subscriber-related information, i.e., Mobile Station International Subscriber Directory Number (MSISDN) was not reported for the iPhone4 GSM, iPhone4 CDMA and the Palm Pre2 for test case SPT-05.

Equipment-related information, i.e., the Mobile Equipment Identity (MEID) was not reported for the iPhone4 CDMA and Palm Pre2.

3.3 Acquisition of Personal Information Management (PIM) data

For test case SPT-06, Personal Information Management (PIM) data i.e., calendar entries, and memos was not reported for the HTC Thunderbolt and the Palm Pre2.

Address book entries were not reported for the Palm Pre2.

Graphics files associated with address book entries were not reported for the iPhone4 GSM, BlackBerry Torch, and iPhone4 CDMA devices.

3.4 Acquisition of call log data

For test case SPT-07, incoming, outgoing and missed calls were not reported for the Palm Pre2.

Missed calls were categorized as Incoming for the iPhone4 GSM and the iPhone4 CDMA.

3.5 Acquisition of SMS messages

For test case SPT-08, Unread text messages were not assigned a status (i.e., Unread) for the iPhone4 GSM and the iPhone4 CDMA devices.

SMS messages were not reported for the Palm Pre2.

3.6 Acquisition of MMS messages

MMS messages were not reported for the Palm Pre2 for test case SPT-09.

MMS attachments (i.e., audio, graphic, video) were not reported for the BlackBerry Torch.

MMS attachments (i.e., audio) were not reported for the iPhone4 GSM and the iPhone4 CDMA.

The textual portion of MMS messages for the iPhone4 CDMA was not reported in the message preview pane. The sms.db file has to be searched.

3.7 Acquisition of stand-alone files

Audio and video files were not reported for the iPhone4 GSM or the iPhone4 CDMA devices for test case SPT-10.

Audio, video and graphic files were not reported for the BlackBerry Torch, HTC Thunderbolt, and Palm Pre2.

3.8 Acquisition of application-related data

For test case SPT-11, application-related data (e.g., Quickoffice documents) were not reported for the HTC Thunderbolt or the Palm Pre2.

3.9 Acquisition of Internet-related data

For test case SPT-12 Internet-related data (i.e., bookmarks, visited sites) was not reported for the Palm Pre2.

3.10 Acquisition of text messages containing non-ASCII characters

For test case SPT-33, contact entries containing Chinese characters were not reported for the BlackBerry Torch, and in text messages containing the 'é' character, it was reported as '|'.

4 Testing Environment

The tests were run in the NIST CFTT lab. This section describes the testing environment, including available computers, mobile devices, and the data objects used to populate mobile devices and SIMs.

4.1 Test computers

One computer was used to run the tool: **Morrisy**.

Morrisy has the following configuration:

Intel® D975XBX2 Motherboard
BIOS Version BX97520J.86A.2674.2007.0315.1546
Intel® Core™ 2 Duo CPU 6700 @ 2.66 Ghz
3.25 GB RAM
1.44 MB floppy drive
LITE–ON CD H LH–52N1P
LITE–ON DVDRW LH–20A1P
2 slots for removable SATA hard disk drive
8 USB 2.0 slots
2 IEEE 1394 ports
3 IEEE 1394 ports (mini)

4.2 Mobile devices

The following table lists the mobile devices used.

Table 4.2 Mobile Devices

Make	Model	OS	Network
Apple iPhone	4	iOS v4.3.3 (8J2)	AT&T
BlackBerry	9800 (Torch)	BlackBerry v6.0.0.526	AT&T
Nokia	6350	V13.1709-12-10 RM-455	AT&T
Apple iPhone	4	iOS v5.0.1 (9A405)	Verizon
HTC	Thunderbolt	Android 2.2.1	Verizon
Palm	Pre2	Palm OS	Verizon

4.3 Internal memory data objects

The following data objects were used to populate the internal memory of the Smart Phones.

Table 4.3 Internal Memory data objects

Data Objects	Data Elements
Address Book Entries	
	Regular Length
	Maximum Length
	Special Character
	Blank Name
	Regular Length, email
	Regular Length, graphic
	Deleted Entry
	Non-ASCII Entry
PIM Data	

Data Objects	Data Elements
	Regular Length
	Maximum Length
	Deleted Entry
	Special Character
Call Logs	
	Incoming
	Outgoing
	Missed
	Incoming - Deleted
	Outgoing - Deleted
	Missed - Deleted
Text Messages	
	Incoming SMS - Read
	Incoming SMS - Unread
	Outgoing SMS
	Incoming EMS - Read
	Incoming EMS - Unread
	Outgoing EMS
	Incoming SMS - Deleted
	Outgoing SMS - Deleted
	Incoming EMS - Deleted
	Outgoing EMS - Deleted
	Non-ASCII EMS
MMS Messages	
	Incoming Audio
	Incoming Graphic
	Incoming Video
	Outgoing Audio
	Outgoing Graphic
	Outgoing Video
Stand-alone data files	
	Audio
	Graphic
	Video
	Audio - Deleted
	Graphic - Deleted
	Video - Deleted
Application Data	
	Device Specific App Data
Location Data	
	GPS Coordinates

4.4 Subscriber Identity Module (SIM) data objects

The following data objects were used to populate the subscriber identity modules.

Table 4.4 Subscriber Identity Module (SIM) Data Objects

Data Objects	Data Elements
Abbreviated Dialing Numbers (ADN)	
	Maximum Length
	Special Character
	Blank Name
	Non-ASCII Entry
	Regular Length - Deleted Number
Call Logs	
	Last Numbers Dialed (LND)
Text Messages	
	Incoming SMS - Read
	Incoming SMS - Unread
	Non-ASCII SMS
	Incoming SMS - Deleted
	Non-ASCII EMS
	Incoming EMS - Deleted

5 Test Results

The main item of interest for interpreting the test results is determining the conformance of the tool with the test assertions. Conformance with each assertion tested by a given test case is evaluated by examining the **Log Highlights** box of the test report.

5.1 Test results report key

The following table presents an explanation of each section of the test details in section 5.2. The Tester Name, Test Host, Test Date, Device, Source Setup, and Log Highlights sections for each test case are populated by excerpts taken from the log files produced by the tool under test.

Table 5 Test Results Report Key

Heading	Description
First Line:	Test case ID, name, and version of tool tested.
Case Summary:	Test case summary from *Smart Phone Tool Test Assertion and Test Plan*.
Assertions:	The test assertions applicable to the test case, selected from *Smart Phone Tool Test Assertion and Test Plan*.
Tester Name:	Name or initials of person executing test procedure.
Test Host:	Host computer executing the test.
Test Date:	Time and date that test was started.

Heading	Description
Device:	Source mobile device, SIM.
Source Setup:	Acquisition interface.
Log Highlights:	Information extracted from various log files to illustrate conformance or nonconformance to the test assertions.
Results:	Expected and actual results for each assertion tested.
Analysis:	Whether or not the expected results were achieved.

5.2 Test details

The test results are presented in this section.

5.2.1 SPT-01 (iPhone4 GSM)

Test Case SPT-01 Device Seizure 5.0 build 4582.15907	
Case Summary:	SPT-01 Acquire mobile device internal memory over tool-supported interfaces (e.g., cable, Bluetooth, IrDA).
Assertions:	SPT-CA-01 If a cellular forensic tool provides support for connectivity of the target device, then the tool shall successfully recognize the target device via all vendor supported interfaces (e.g., cable, Bluetooth, IrDA). SPT-CA-04 If a cellular forensic tool completes acquisition of the target device without error, then the tool shall have the ability to present acquired data objects in a useable format via either a preview pane or generated report. SPT-CA-29 If a cellular forensic tool provides the user with an "Acquire All" device data objects acquisition option, then the tool shall complete the acquisition of all data objects without error. SPT-CA-30 If a cellular forensic tool provides the user with a "Select All" individual device data objects, then the tool shall complete the acquisition of all individually selected data objects without error. SPT-CA-31 If a cellular forensic tool provides the user with the ability to "Select Individual" device data objects for acquisition, then the tool shall acquire each exclusive data object without error. SPT-CA-32 If a cellular forensic tool completes two consecutive logical acquisitions of the target device without error, then the payload (data objects) on the mobile device shall remain consistent.
Tester Name:	rpa
Test Host:	Morrisy
Test Date:	Fri Sep 21 12:18:32 EDT 2012
Device:	iPhone4_GSM
Source Setup:	OS: WIN XP v5.1.2600 Interface: cable
Log Highlights:	Created by Device Seizure v5.0 Acquisition started: Fri Sep 21 12:18:32 EDT 2012 Acquisition finished: Fri Sep 21 12:22:57 EDT 2012

Device connectivity was established via supported interface |

Results:

Assertion & Expected Result	Actual Result
SPT-CA-01 Device connectivity via supported interfaces.	as expected
SPT-CA-04 Readability and completeness of acquired data via supported reports.	as expected
SPT-CA-29 Acquire - All data objects acquisition.	as expected
SPT-CA-30 Select - All data objects acquisition.	as expected
SPT-CA-31 Select - Individual data objects acquisition.	as expected
SPT-CA-32 Perform back-to-back acquisitions, check device payload for modifications.	as expected

Test Case SPT-01 Device Seizure 5.0 build 4582.15907	
Analysis:	Expected results achieved

5.2.2 SPT-02 (iPhone4 GSM)

Test Case SPT-02 Device Seizure 5.0 build 4582.15907	
Case Summary:	SPT-02 Attempt internal memory acquisition of a nonsupported mobile device.
Assertions:	SPT-CA-02 If a cellular forensic tool attempts to connect to a nonsupported device, then the tool shall notify the user that the device is not supported.
Tester Name:	rpa
Test Host:	Morrisy
Test Date:	Fri Sep 21 12:24:09 EDT 2012
Device:	unsupported_device
Source Setup:	OS: WIN XP v5.1.2600 Interface: cable
Log Highlights:	Created by Device Seizure v5.0 Acquisition started: Fri Sep 21 12:24:09 EDT 2012 Acquisition finished: Fri Sep 21 12:26:05 EDT 2012 Identification of nonsupported devices was successful
Results:	

Assertion & Expected Result	Actual Result
SPT-CA-02 Identification of nonsupported devices.	as expected

Analysis:	Expected results achieved

5.2.3 SPT-03 (iPhone4 GSM)

Test Case SPT-03 Device Seizure 5.0 build 4582.15907	
Case Summary:	SPT-03 Begin mobile device internal memory acquisition and interrupt connectivity by interface disengagement.
Assertions:	SPT-CA-03 If connectivity between the mobile device and cellular forensic tool is disrupted, then the tool shall notify the user that connectivity has been disrupted.
Tester Name:	rpa
Test Host:	Morrisy
Test Date:	Fri Sep 21 12:24:28 EDT 2012
Device:	iPhone4 GSM
Source Setup:	OS: WIN XP v5.1.2600 Interface: cable
Log Highlights:	Created by Device Seizure v5.0 Acquisition started: Fri Sep 21 12:24:28 EDT 2012 Acquisition finished: Fri Sep 21 12:26:18 EDT 2012 Device acquisition disruption notification was successful
Results:	

Assertion & Expected Result	Actual Result
SPT-CA-03 Notification of device acquisition disruption.	as expected

Analysis:	Expected results achieved

5.2.4 SPT-04 (iPhone4 GSM)

Test Case SPT-04 Device Seizure 5.0 build 4582.15907	

Test Case SPT-04 Device Seizure 5.0 build 4582.15907	
Case Summary:	SPT-04 Acquire mobile device internal memory and review reported data via the preview pane or generated reports for readability.
Assertions:	SPT-CA-04 If a cellular forensic tool completes acquisition of the target device without error, then the tool shall have the ability to present acquired data objects in a useable format via either a preview pane or generated report.
Tester Name:	rpa
Test Host:	Morrisy
Test Date:	Fri Sep 21 12:28:23 EDT 2012
Device:	iPhone4_GSM
Source Setup:	OS: WIN XP v5.1.2600 Interface: cable
Log Highlights:	Created by Device Seizure v5.0 Acquisition started: Fri Sep 21 12:28:23 EDT 2012 Acquisition finished: Fri Sep 21 12:29:25 EDT 2012 Readability and completeness of acquired data was successful
Results:	

Assertion & Expected Result	Actual Result
SPT-CA-04 Readability and completeness of acquired data via supported reports.	as expected

Analysis:	Expected results achieved

5.2.5 SPT-05 (iPhone4 GSM)

Test Case SPT-05 Device Seizure 5.0 build 4582.15907	
Case Summary:	SPT-05 Acquire mobile device internal memory and review reported subscriber and equipment-related information (e.g., IMEI/MEID/ESN, MSISDN).
Assertions:	SPT-CA-05 If a cellular forensic tool completes acquisition of the target device without error, then subscriber related information shall be presented in a useable format. SPT-CA-06 If a cellular forensic tool completes acquisition of the target device without error, then equipment-related information shall be presented in a useable format.
Tester Name:	rpa
Test Host:	Morrisy
Test Date:	Fri Sep 21 12:29:49 EDT 2012
Device:	iPhone4 GSM
Source Setup:	OS: WIN XP v5.1.2600 Interface: cable
Log Highlights:	Created by Device Seizure v5.0 Acquisition started: Fri Sep 21 12:29:49 EDT 2012 Acquisition finished: Fri Sep 21 12:32:54 EDT 2012 IMEI was acquired **Notes:** MSISDN was not reported
Results:	

Assertion & Expected Result	Actual Result
SPT-CA-05 Acquisition of MSISDN, IMSI.	Not as expected
SPT-CA-06 Acquisition of IMEI/MEID/ESN.	as expected

Analysis:	Partial results achieved

5.2.6 SPT-06 (iPhone4 GSM)

Test Case SPT-06 Device Seizure 5.0 build 4582.15907	
Case Summary:	SPT-06 Acquire mobile device internal memory and review reported PIM-related data.
Assertions:	SPT-CA-07 If a cellular forensic tool completes acquisition of the target device without error, then address book entries shall be presented in a useable format. SPT-CA-08 If a cellular forensic tool completes acquisition of the target device without error, then maximum length address book entries shall be presented in a useable format. SPT-CA-09 If a cellular forensic tool completes acquisition of the target device without error, then address book entries containing special characters shall be presented in a useable format. SPT-CA-10 If a cellular forensic tool completes acquisition of the target device without error, then address book entries containing blank names shall be presented in a useable format. SPT-CA-11 If a cellular forensic tool completes acquisition of the target device without error, then email addresses associated with address book entries shall be presented in a useable format. SPT-CA-12 If a cellular forensic tool completes acquisition of the target device without error, then graphics associated with address book entries shall be presented in a useable format. SPT-CA-13 If a cellular forensic tool completes acquisition of the target device without error, then datebook, calendar, note entries shall be presented in a useable format. SPT-CA-14 If a cellular forensic tool completes acquisition of the target device without error, then maximum length datebook, calendar, note entries shall be presented in a useable format.
Tester Name:	rpa
Test Host:	Morrisy
Test Date:	Fri Sep 21 12:34:14 EDT 2012
Device:	iPhone4 GSM
Source Setup:	OS: WIN XP v5.1.2600 Interface: cable
Log Highlights:	Created by Device Seizure v5.0 Acquisition started: Fri Sep 21 12:34:14 EDT 2012 Acquisition finished: Fri Sep 21 12:46:12 EDT 2012 Regular Length Address Book entries were acquired Maximum Length Address Book entries were acquired Special Character Address Book entries were acquired Blank Name Address Book entries were acquired Email addresses within Address Book entries were acquired Embedded graphics within Address Book entries were not acquired ALL PIM-related data was acquired **Notes:** Graphics files associated with address book entries were not reported.

Results:		
	Assertion & Expected Result	**Actual Result**
	SPT-CA-07 Acquisition of address book entries.	as expected
	SPT-CA-08 Acquisition of maximum length address book entries.	as expected
	SPT-CA-09 Acquisition of address book entries containing special characters.	as expected
	SPT-CA-10 Acquisition of address book entries containing a blank name entry.	as expected
	SPT-CA-11 Acquisition of embedded email addresses within address book entries.	as expected
	SPT-CA-12 Acquisition of embedded graphics within address book entries.	Not as expected
	SPT-CA-13 Acquisition of PIM data (i.e., datebook/calendar, notes).	as expected
	SPT-CA-14 Acquisition of maximum length PIM data.	as expected

Test Case SPT-06 Device Seizure 5.0 build 4582.15907	
Analysis:	Partial results achieved

5.2.7 SPT-07 (iPhone4 GSM)

Test Case SPT-07 Device Seizure 5.0 build 4582.15907	
Case Summary:	SPT-07 Acquire mobile device internal memory and review reported call logs.
Assertions:	SPT-CA-15 If a cellular forensic tool completes acquisition of the target device without error, then call logs (incoming/outgoing/missed) shall be presented in a useable format. SPT-CA-16 If a cellular forensic tool completes acquisition of the target device without error, then the corresponding date/time stamps and the duration of the call for call logs shall be presented in a useable format.
Tester Name:	rpa
Test Host:	Morrisy
Test Date:	Fri Sep 21 12:48:48 EDT 2012
Device:	iPhone4 GSM
Source Setup:	OS: WIN XP v5.1.2600 Interface: cable
Log Highlights:	Created by Device Seizure v5.0 Acquisition started: Fri Sep 21 12:48:48 EDT 2012 Acquisition finished: Fri Sep 21 12:57:17 EDT 2012 All Call Logs (incoming, outgoing, missed) were acquired All Call Log date/time stamps data were correctly reported **Notes**: Missed calls were categorized as Incoming calls.
Results:	

Assertion & Expected Result	Actual Result
SPT-CA-15 Acquisition of call logs.	Not as expected
SPT-CA-16 Acquisition of call log date/time stamps.	as expected

Analysis:	Partial results achieved

5.2.8 SPT-08 (iPhone4 GSM)

Test Case SPT-08 Device Seizure 5.0 build 4582.15907	
Case Summary:	SPT-08 Acquire mobile device internal memory and review reported text messages.
Assertions:	SPT-CA-17 If a cellular forensic tool completes acquisition of the target device without error, then ASCII text messages (i.e., SMS, EMS) shall be presented in a useable format. SPT-CA-18 If a cellular forensic tool completes acquisition of the target device without error, then the corresponding date/time stamps for text messages shall be presented in a useable format. SPT-CA-19 If a cellular forensic tool completes acquisition of the target device without error, then the corresponding status (i.e., read, unread) for text messages shall be presented in a useable format. SPT-CA-20 If a cellular forensic tool completes acquisition of the target device without error, then the corresponding sender / recipient phone numbers for text messages shall be presented in a useable format.
Tester Name:	rpa
Test Host:	Morrisy
Test Date:	Fri Sep 21 12:49:18 EDT 2012
Device:	iPhone4 GSM
Source Setup:	OS: WIN XP v5.1.2600 Interface: cable

Test Case SPT-08 Device Seizure 5.0 build 4582.15907		
Log Highlights:	Created by Device Seizure v5.0 Acquisition started: Fri Sep 21 12:49:18 EDT 2012 Acquisition finished: Fri Sep 21 13:05:16 EDT 2012 ALL text messages (SMS, EMS) were acquired Correct date/time stamps were reported for all text messages Partial status flags were reported for all text messages Sender and Recipient phone numbers associated with text messages were correctly reported **Notes**: Unread text messages were not assigned a Type i.e., UNREAD	
Results:		

Assertion & Expected Result	Actual Result
SPT-CA-17 Acquisition of text messages.	as expected
SPT-CA-18 Acquisition of text message date/time stamps.	as expected
SPT-CA-19 Acquisition of text message status flags.	Not as expected
SPT-CA-20 Acquisition of sender/recipient phone number associated with text messages.	as expected

Analysis:	Partial results achieved

5.2.9 SPT-09 (iPhone4 GSM)

Test Case SPT-09 Device Seizure 5.0 build 4582.15907	
Case Summary:	SPT-09 Acquire mobile device internal memory and review reported MMS multi-media-related data (i.e., text, audio, graphics, video).
Assertions:	SPT-CA-21 If a cellular forensic tool completes acquisition of the target device without error, then MMS messages and associated audio shall be presented in a useable format. SPT-CA-22 If a cellular forensic tool completes acquisition of the target device without error, then MMS messages and associated graphic files shall be presented in a useable format. SPT-CA-23 If a cellular forensic tool completes acquisition of the target device without error, then MMS messages and associated video shall be presented in a useable format.
Tester Name:	rpa
Test Host:	Morrisy
Test Date:	Fri Sep 21 13:08:08 EDT 2012
Device:	iPhone4_GSM
Source Setup:	OS: WIN XP v5.1.2600 Interface: cable
Log Highlights:	Created by Device Seizure v5.0 Acquisition started: Fri Sep 21 13:08:08 EDT 2012 Acquisition finished: Fri Sep 21 13:38:56 EDT 2012 Partial audio MMS messages were acquired Image MMS messages were acquired Video MMS messages were acquired **Notes**: Sound bytes attached to MMS messages were not reported. The textual portion of the MMS messages is blank and has to be searched for in the sms.db file.
Results:	

Assertion & Expected Result	Actual Result
SPT-CA-21 Acquisition of audio MMS messages.	Not as expected
SPT-CA-22 Acquisition of graphic data image MMS	as expected

Test Case SPT-09 Device Seizure 5.0 build 4582.15907		
	messages.	
	SPT-CA-23 Acquisition of video MMS messages.	as expected
Analysis:	Partial results achieved	

5.2.10 SPT-10 (iPhone4 GSM)

Test Case SPT-10 Device Seizure 5.0 build 4582.15907	
Case Summary:	SPT-10 Acquire mobile device internal memory and review reported stand-alone multi-media data (i.e., audio, graphics, video).
Assertions:	SPT-CA-24 If a cellular forensic tool completes acquisition of the target device without error, then stand-alone audio files shall be presented in a useable format via either an internal application or suggested third-party application. SPT-CA-25 If a cellular forensic tool completes acquisition of the target device without error, then stand-alone graphic files shall be presented in a useable format via either an internal application or suggested third-party application. SPT-CA-26 If a cellular forensic tool completes acquisition of the target device without error, then stand-alone video files shall be presented in a useable format via either an internal application or suggested third-party application.
Tester Name:	rpa
Test Host:	Morrisy
Test Date:	Fri Sep 21 13:54:13 EDT 2012
Device:	iPhone4 GSM
Source Setup:	OS: WIN XP v5.1.2600 Interface: cable
Log Highlights:	Created by Device Seizure v5.0 Acquisition started: Fri Sep 21 13:54:13 EDT 2012 Acquisition finished: Fri Sep 21 13:55:38 EDT 2012 Audio files were not acquired Image files were acquired Video files were not acquired
Results:	

Assertion & Expected Result	Actual Result
SPT-CA-24 Acquisition of stand-alone audio files.	Not as expected
SPT-CA-25 Acquisition of stand-alone graphic files.	as expected
SPT-CA-26 Acquisition of stand-alone video files.	Not as expected

Analysis:	Expected results achieved

5.2.11 SPT-12 (iPhone4 GSM)

Test Case SPT-12 Device Seizure 5.0 build 4582.15907	
Case Summary:	SPT-12 Acquire mobile device internal memory and review Internet-related data (i.e., bookmarks, visited sites.
Assertions:	SPT-CA-28 If a cellular forensic tool completes acquisition of the target device without error, then Internet-related data (i.e., bookmarks, visited sites) cached to the device shall be acquired and presented in a useable format.
Tester Name:	rpa
Test Host:	Morrisy
Test Date:	Fri Sep 21 13:55:28 EDT 2012
Device:	iPhone4 GSM
Source Setup:	OS: WIN XP v5.1.2600 Interface: cable

Test Case SPT-12 Device Seizure 5.0 build 4582.15907	
Log Highlights:	Created by Device Seizure v5.0 Acquisition started: Fri Sep 21 13:55:28 EDT 2012 Acquisition finished: Fri Sep 21 14:04:11 EDT 2012 All Internet-related data was acquired
Results:	

Assertion & Expected Result	Actual Result
SPT-CA-28 Acquisition of Internet-related data.	as expected

Analysis:	Expected results achieved

5.2.12 SPT-13 (iPhone4 GSM)

Test Case SPT-13 Device Seizure 5.0 build 4582.15907	
Case Summary:	SPT-13 Acquire mobile device internal memory by selecting a combination of supported data elements.
Assertions:	SPT-CA-29 If a cellular forensic tool provides the user with an "Acquire All" device data objects acquisition option, then the tool shall complete the acquisition of all data objects without error. SPT-CA-30 If a cellular forensic tool provides the user with an "Select All" individual device data objects, then the tool shall complete the acquisition of all individually selected data objects without error. SPT-CA-31 If a cellular forensic tool provides the user with the ability to "Select Individual" device data objects for acquisition, then the tool shall acquire each exclusive data object without error.
Tester Name:	rpa
Test Host:	Morrisy
Test Date:	Fri Sep 21 13:07:27 EDT 2012
Device:	iPhone4 GSM
Source Setup:	OS: WIN XP v5.1.2600 Interface: cable
Log Highlights:	Created by Device Seizure v5.0 Acquisition started: Fri Sep 21 13:07:27 EDT 2012 Acquisition finished: Fri Sep 21 13:17:42 EDT 2012 Acquire All acquisition was successful
Results:	

Assertion & Expected Result	Actual Result
SPT-CA-29 Acquire-All data objects acquisition.	as expected
SPT-CA-30 Select-All data objects acquisition.	as expected
SPT-CA-31 Select-Individual data objects acquisition.	as expected

Analysis:	Expected results achieved

5.2.13 SPT-14 (iPhone4 GSM)

Test Case SPT-14 Device Seizure 5.0 build 4582.15907	
Case Summary:	SPT-14 Acquire SIM memory over supported interfaces (e.g., PC/SC reader).
Assertions:	SPT-AO-01 If a cellular forensic tool provides support for connectivity of the target SIM, then the tool shall successfully recognize the target SIM via all tool-supported interfaces (e.g., PC/SC reader, proprietary reader, Smart Phone itself).
Tester Name:	rpa
Test Host:	Morrisy
Test Date:	Fri Sep 21 14:17:30 EDT 2012

Test Case SPT-14 Device Seizure 5.0 build 4582.15907	
Device:	iPhone4 GSM
Source Setup:	OS: WIN XP v5.1.2600 Interface: USB
Log Highlights:	Created by Device Seizure v5.0 Acquisition started: Fri Sep 21 14:17:30 EDT 2012 Acquisition finished: Fri Sep 21 14:26:03 EDT 2012 Media connectivity was established via supported interface
Results:	

Assertion & Expected Result	Actual Result
SPT-AO-01 SIM connectivity via supported interfaces.	as expected

Analysis:	Expected results achieved

5.2.14 SPT-15 (iPhone4 GSM)

Test Case SPT-15 Device Seizure 5.0 build 4582.15907	
Case Summary:	SPT-15 Attempt acquisition of a nonsupported SIM.
Assertions:	SPT-AO-02 If a cellular forensic tool attempts to connect to a nonsupported SIM, then the tool shall notify the user that the SIM is not supported.
Tester Name:	rpa
Test Host:	Morrisy
Test Date:	Fri Sep 21 14:17:48 EDT 2012
Device:	iPhone4 GSM
Source Setup:	OS: WIN XP v5.1.2600 Interface: USB
Log Highlights:	Created by Device Seizure v5.0 Acquisition started: Fri Sep 21 14:17:48 EDT 2012 Acquisition finished: Fri Sep 21 14:26:13 EDT 2012 Identification of nonsupported media was successful
Results:	

Assertion & Expected Result	Actual Result
SPT-AO-02 Identification of nonsupported SIMs.	as expected

Analysis:	Expected results achieved

5.2.15 SPT-16 (iPhone4 GSM)

Test Case SPT-16 Device Seizure 5.0 build 4582.15907	
Case Summary:	SPT-16 Begin SIM acquisition and interrupt connectivity by interface disengagement.
Assertions:	SPT-AO-03 If a cellular forensic tool loses connectivity with the SIM reader, then the tool shall notify the user that connectivity has been disrupted.
Tester Name:	rpa
Test Host:	Morrisy
Test Date:	Fri Sep 21 14:26:46 EDT 2012
Device:	iPhone4 GSM
Source Setup:	OS: WIN XP v5.1.2600 Interface: USB
Log Highlights:	Created by Device Seizure v5.0 Acquisition started: Fri Sep 21 14:26:46 EDT 2012 Acquisition finished: Fri Sep 21 14:32:06 EDT 2012

Test Case SPT-16 Device Seizure 5.0 build 4582.15907	
	Media acquisition disruption notification was successful
Results:	

Assertion & Expected Result	Actual Result
SPT-AO-03 Notification of SIM acquisition disruption.	as expected

Analysis:	Expected results achieved

5.2.16 SPT-17 (iPhone4 GSM)

Test Case SPT-17 Device Seizure 5.0 build 4582.15907	
Case Summary:	SPT-17 Acquire SIM memory and review reported subscriberand equipment-related information (i.e., SPN, ICCID, IMSI, MSISDN).
Assertions:	SPT-AO-04 If a cellular forensic tool completes acquisition of the target SIM without error, then the SPN shall be presented in a useable format. SPT-AO-05 If a cellular forensic tool completes acquisition of the target SIM without error, then the ICCID shall be presented in a useable format. SPT-AO-06 If a cellular forensic tool completes acquisition of the target SIM without error, then the IMSI shall be presented in a useable format. SPT-AO-07 If a cellular forensic tool completes acquisition of the target SIM without error, then the MSISDN shall be presented in a useable format.
Tester Name:	rpa
Test Host:	Morrisy
Test Date:	Fri Sep 21 14:28:13 EDT 2012
Device:	iPhone4 GSM
Source Setup:	OS: WIN XP v5.1.2600 Interface: USB
Log Highlights:	Created by Device Seizure v5.0 Acquisition started: Fri Sep 21 14:28:13 EDT 2012 Acquisition finished: Fri Sep 21 14:32:13 EDT 2012 All subscriber related data (i.e., SPN, ICCID, IMSI, MSISDN) was acquired
Results:	

Assertion & Expected Result	Actual Result
SPT-AO-04 Acquisition of SPN.	as expected
SPT-AO-05 Acquisition of ICCID.	as expected
SPT-AO-06 Acquisition of IMSI.	as expected
SPT-AO-07 Acquisition of MSISDN.	as expected

Analysis:	Expected results achieved

5.2.17 SPT-18 (iPhone4 GSM)

Test Case SPT-18 Device Seizure 5.0 build 4582.15907	
Case Summary:	SPT-18 Acquire SIM memory and review reported Abbreviated Dialing Numbers (ADN).
Assertions:	SPT-AO-08 If a cellular forensic tool completes acquisition of the target SIM without error, then ASCII Abbreviated Dialing Numbers (ADN) shall be presented in a useable format. SPT-AO-09 If a cellular forensic tool completes acquisition of the target SIM without error, then maximum length ADNs shall be presented in a useable format. SPT-AO-10 If a cellular forensic tool completes acquisition of the SIM without error, then ADNs containing special characters shall be presented in a useable format. SPT-AO-11 If a cellular forensic tool completes acquisition of the SIM without error, then ADNs containing blank names shall be presented in a useable format.
Tester Name:	rpa

Test Case SPT-18 Device Seizure 5.0 build 4582.15907	
Test Host:	Morrisy
Test Date:	Fri Sep 21 14:28:28 EDT 2012
Device:	iPhone4 GSM
Source Setup:	OS: WIN XP v5.1.2600 Interface: USB
Log Highlights:	Created by Device Seizure v5.0 Acquisition started: Fri Sep 21 14:28:28 EDT 2012 Acquisition finished: Fri Sep 21 14:32:19 EDT 2012 All ADNs were acquired
Results:	

Assertion & Expected Result	Actual Result
SPT-AO-08 Acquisition of ADNs.	as expected
SPT-AO-09 Acquisition of maximum length ADNs.	as expected
SPT-AO-10 Acquisition of special character ADNs.	as expected
SPT-AO-11 Acquisition of blank name ADNs.	as expected

Analysis:	Expected results achieved

5.2.18 SPT-19 (iPhone4 GSM)

Test Case SPT-19 Device Seizure 5.0 build 4582.15907	
Case Summary:	SPT-19 Acquire SIM memory and review reported Last Numbers Dialed (LND).
Assertions:	SPT-AO-12 If a cellular forensic tool completes acquisition of the target SIM without error, then Last Numbers Dialed (LND) shall be presented in a useable format. SPT-AO-13 If a cellular forensic tool completes acquisition of the target SIM without error, then the corresponding date/time stamps for LNDs shall be presented in a useable format.
Tester Name:	rpa
Test Host:	Morrisy
Test Date:	Fri Sep 21 14:28:43 EDT 2012
Device:	iPhone4 GSM
Source Setup:	OS: WIN XP v5.1.2600 Interface: USB
Log Highlights:	Created by Device Seizure v5.0 Acquisition started: Fri Sep 21 14:28:43 EDT 2012 Acquisition finished: Fri Sep 21 14:32:26 EDT 2012 LNDs were acquired Date/Time Stamps correctly reported for LNDs
Results:	

Assertion & Expected Result	Actual Result
SPT-AO-12 Acquisition of LNDs.	as expected
SPT-AO-13 Acquisition of LND date/time stamps.	as expected

Analysis:	Expected results achieved

5.2.19 SPT-20 (iPhone4 GSM)

Test Case SPT-20 Device Seizure 5.0 build 4582.15907	
Case Summary:	SPT-20 Acquire SIM memory and review reported text messages (SMS, EMS).
Assertions:	SPT-AO-14 If a cellular forensic tool completes acquisition of the target SIM without error, then ASCII SMS text messages shall be presented in a useable format. SPT-AO-15 If a cellular forensic tool completes acquisition of the target

Test Case SPT-20 Device Seizure 5.0 build 4582.15907	
	SIM without error, then ASCII EMS text messages shall be presented in a useable format. SPT-AO-16 If a cellular forensic tool completes acquisition of the target SIM without error, then the corresponding date/time stamps for all text messages shall be presented in a useable format. SPT-AO-17 If a cellular forensic tool completes acquisition of the target SIM without error, then the corresponding status (i.e., read, unread) for text messages shall be presented in a useable format. SPT-AO-18 If a cellular forensic tool completes acquisition of the target SIM without error, then the corresponding sender / recipient phone numbers for text messages shall be presented in a useable format.
Tester Name:	rpa
Test Host:	Morrisy
Test Date:	Fri Sep 21 14:29:02 EDT 2012
Device:	iPhone4_GSM
Source Setup:	OS: WIN XP v5.1.2600 Interface: USB
Log Highlights:	Created by Device Seizure v5.0 Acquisition started: Fri Sep 21 14:29:02 EDT 2012 Acquisition finished: Fri Sep 21 14:32:37 EDT 2012 ALL text messages (SMS, EMS) were acquired All date/time stamps were reported for text messages Correct status flags were reported for text messages Sender and Recipient phone numbers associated with text messages were correctly reported
Results:	

Assertion & Expected Result	Actual Result
SPT-AO-14 Acquisition of SMS messages.	as expected
SPT-AO-15 Acquisition of EMS messages.	as expected
SPT-AO-16 Acquisition of text message date/time stamps.	as expected
SPT-AO-17 Acquisition of text message status flags.	as expected
SPT-AO-18 Acquisition of sender/recipient phone number associated with text messages.	as expected

Analysis:	Expected results achieved

5.2.20 SPT-21 (iPhone4 GSM)

Test Case SPT-21 Device Seizure 5.0 build 4582.15907	
Case Summary:	SPT-21 Acquire SIM memory and review recoverable deleted text messages (SMS, EMS).
Assertions:	SPT-AO-19 If the cellular forensic tool completes acquisition of the target SIM without error, then deleted text messages that have not been overwritten shall be presented in a useable format.
Tester Name:	rpa
Test Host:	Morrisy
Test Date:	Fri Sep 21 14:29:16 EDT 2012
Device:	iPhone4_GSM
Source Setup:	OS: WIN XP v5.1.2600 Interface: USB
Log Highlights:	Created by Device Seizure v5.0 Acquisition started: Fri Sep 21 14:29:16 EDT 2012 Acquisition finished: Fri Sep 21 14:32:43 EDT 2012 Deleted text message data was recovered
Results:	

Assertion & Expected Result	Actual Result

Test Case SPT-21 Device Seizure 5.0 build 4582.15907		
	SPT-AO-19 Acquisition of non-overwritten deleted text messages.	as expected
Analysis:	Expected results achieved	

5.2.21 SPT-22 (iPhone4 GSM)

Test Case SPT-22 Device Seizure 5.0 build 4582.15907	
Case Summary:	SPT-22 Acquire SIM memory and review reported location-related data (i.e., LOCI, GPRSLOCI).
Assertions:	SPT-AO-20 If a cellular forensic tool completes acquisition of the target SIM without error, then location-related data (i.e., LOCI) shall be presented in a useable format. SPT-AO-21 If a cellular forensic tool completes acquisition of the target SIM without error, then location-related data (i.e., GRPSLOCI) shall be presented in a useable format.
Tester Name:	rpa
Test Host:	Morrisy
Test Date:	Fri Sep 21 14:29:33 EDT 2012
Device:	iPhone4 GSM
Source Setup:	OS: WIN XP v5.1.2600 Interface: USB
Log Highlights:	Created by Device Seizure v5.0 Acquisition started: Fri Sep 21 14:29:33 EDT 2012 Acquisition finished: Fri Sep 21 14:32:52 EDT 2012 LOCI data was acquired GPRSLOCI data was acquired
Results:	

Assertion & Expected Result	Actual Result
SPT-AO-20 Acquisition of LOCI information.	as expected
SPT-AO-21 Acquisition of GPRSLOCI information.	as expected

Analysis:	Expected results achieved

5.2.22 SPT-23 (iPhone4 GSM)

Test Case SPT-23 Device Seizure 5.0 build 4582.15907	
Case Summary:	SPT-23 Acquire SIM memory by selecting a combination of supported data elements.
Assertions:	SPT-AO-01 If a cellular forensic tool provides support for connectivity of the target SIM, then the tool shall successfully recognize the target SIM via all tool-supported interfaces (e.g., PC/SC reader, proprietary reader, Smart Phone itself). SPT-AO-22 If a cellular forensic tool provides the user with an "Acquire All" SIM data objects acquisition option, then the tool shall complete the acquisition of all data objects without error. SPT-AO-23 If a cellular forensic tool provides the user with an "Select All" individual SIM data objects, then the tool shall complete the acquisition of all individually selected data objects without error. SPT-AO-24 If a cellular forensic tool provides the user with the ability to "Select Individual" SIM data objects for acquisition, then the tool shall acquire each exclusive data object without error.
Tester Name:	rpa
Test Host:	Morrisy
Test Date:	Fri Sep 21 14:29:47 EDT 2012
Device:	iPhone4 GSM
Source	OS: WIN XP v5.1.2600

Test Case SPT-23 Device Seizure 5.0 build 4582.15907	
Setup:	Interface: USB
Log Highlights:	Created by Device Seizure v5.0 Acquisition started: Fri Sep 21 14:29:47 EDT 2012 Acquisition finished: Fri Sep 21 14:32:58 EDT 2012 Acquire All acquisition was successful
Results:	

Assertion & Expected Result	Actual Result
SPT-AO-01 SIM connectivity via supported interfaces.	as expected
SPT-AO-22 Acquire-All data objects acquisition.	as expected
SPT-AO-23 Select-All data objects acquisition.	as expected
SPT-AO-24 Select-Individual data objects acquisition.	as expected

Analysis:	Expected results achieved

5.2.23 SPT-24 (iPhone4 GSM)

Test Case SPT-24 Device Seizure 5.0 build 4582.15907	
Case Summary:	SPT-24 Acquire mobile device internal memory and review reported data via supported generated report formats.
Assertions:	SPT-AO-25 If a cellular forensic tool completes acquisition of the target device without error, then the tool shall present the acquired data in a useable format via supported generated report formats.
Tester Name:	rpa
Test Host:	Morrisy
Test Date:	Fri Sep 21 14:35:14 EDT 2012
Device:	iPhone4 GSM
Source Setup:	OS: WIN XP v5.1.2600 Interface: cable
Log Highlights:	Created by Device Seizure v5.0 Acquisition started: Fri Sep 21 14:35:14 EDT 2012 Acquisition finished: Fri Sep 21 14:37:44 EDT 2012 Complete representation of known data via generated reports was successful
Results:	

Assertion & Expected Result	Actual Result
SPT-AO-25 Comparison of known device data elements via generated reports.	as expected

Analysis:	Expected results achieved

5.2.24 SPT-25 (iPhone4 GSM)

Test Case SPT-25 Device Seizure 5.0 build 4582.15907	
Case Summary:	SPT-25 Acquire mobile device internal memory and review reported data via the preview pane.
Assertions:	SPT-AO-26 If a cellular forensic tool completes acquisition of the target device without error, then the tool shall present the acquired data in a useable format in a preview pane view.
Tester Name:	rpa
Test Host:	Morrisy
Test Date:	Fri Sep 21 14:35:30 EDT 2012
Device:	iPhone4 GSM
Source Setup:	OS: WIN XP v5.1.2600 Interface: cable

Test Case SPT-25 Device Seizure 5.0 build 4582.15907	
Log Highlights:	Created by Device Seizure v5.0 Acquisition started: Fri Sep 21 14:35:30 EDT 2012 Acquisition finished: Fri Sep 21 14:37:53 EDT 2012 Complete representation of known data via preview pane was successful
Results:	

Assertion & Expected Result	Actual Result
SPT-AO-26 Comparison of known device data elements via preview pane.	as expected

Analysis:	Expected results achieved

5.2.25 SPT-26 (iPhone4 GSM)

Test Case SPT-26 Device Seizure 5.0 build 4582.15907	
Case Summary:	SPT-26 Acquire SIM memory and review reported data via supported generated report formats.
Assertions:	SPT-AO-25 If a cellular forensic tool completes acquisition of the SIM without error, then the tool shall present the acquired data in a useable format via supported generated report formats.
Tester Name:	rpa
Test Host:	Morrisy
Test Date:	Fri Sep 21 14:35:49 EDT 2012
Device:	iPhone4_GSM
Source Setup:	OS: WIN XP v5.1.2600 Interface: USB
Log Highlights:	Created by Device Seizure v5.0 Acquisition started: Fri Sep 21 14:35:49 EDT 2012 Acquisition finished: Fri Sep 21 14:38:17 EDT 2012 Complete representation of known data via generated reports was successful
Results:	

Assertion & Expected Result	Actual Result
SPT-AO-25 Comparison of known device data elements via generated reports.	as expected

Analysis:	Expected results achieved

5.2.26 SPT-27 (iPhone4 GSM)

Test Case SPT-27 Device Seizure 5.0 build 4582.15907	
Case Summary:	SPT-27 Acquire SIM memory and review reported data via the preview pane.
Assertions:	SPT-AO-26 If a cellular forensic tool completes acquisition of the SIM without error, then the tool shall present the acquired data in a useable format in a preview pane view.
Tester Name:	rpa
Test Host:	Morrisy
Test Date:	Fri Sep 21 14:36:05 EDT 2012
Device:	iPhone4_GSM
Source Setup:	OS: WIN XP v5.1.2600 Interface: USB
Log Highlights:	Created by Device Seizure v5.0 Acquisition started: Fri Sep 21 14:36:05 EDT 2012 Acquisition finished: Fri Sep 21 14:38:32 EDT 2012

Test Case SPT-27 Device Seizure 5.0 build 4582.15907		
	Complete representation of known data via preview pane was successful	
Results:		
	Assertion & Expected Result	Actual Result
	SPT-AO-26 Comparison of known device data elements via preview pane.	as expected
Analysis:	Expected results achieved	

5.2.27 SPT-28 (iPhone4 GSM)

Test Case SPT-28 Device Seizure 5.0 build 4582.15907	
Case Summary:	SPT-28 Attempt acquisition of a password-protected SIM.
Assertions:	SPT-AO-28 If the SIM is password-protected, then the cellular forensic tool shall provide the examiner with the opportunity to input the PIN before acquisition.
Tester Name:	rpa
Test Host:	Morrisy
Test Date:	Fri Sep 21 14:48:09 EDT 2012
Device:	iPhone4 GSM
Source Setup:	OS: WIN XP v5.1.2600 Interface: USB
Log Highlights:	Created by Device Seizure v5.0 Acquisition started: Fri Sep 21 14:48:09 EDT 2012 Acquisition finished: Fri Sep 21 14:49:05 EDT 2012 Ability to enter PIN on protected media before acquisition was successful

Results:		
	Assertion & Expected Result	Actual Result
	SPT-AO-28 Acquisition of password-protected SIM.	as expected
Analysis:	Expected results achieved	

5.2.28 SPT-29 (iPhone4 GSM)

Test Case SPT-29 Device Seizure 5.0 build 4582.15907	
Case Summary:	SPT-29 After a successful mobile device internal memory, alter the case file via third-party means and attempt to reopen the case.
Assertions:	SPT-AO-27 If the case file or individual data objects are modified via third-party means, then the tool shall provide protection mechanisms disallowing or reporting data modification.
Tester Name:	rpa
Test Host:	Morrisy
Test Date:	Fri Sep 21 14:44:53 EDT 2012
Device:	iPhone4_GSM
Source Setup:	OS: WIN XP v5.1.2600 Interface: cable
Log Highlights:	Created by Device Seizure v5.0 Acquisition started: Fri Sep 21 14:44:53 EDT 2012 Acquisition finished: Fri Sep 21 14:47:28 EDT 2012 Notification of modified device memory data was successful

Results:		
	Assertion & Expected Result	Actual Result
	SPT-AO-27 Notification of modified device case data.	as expected

Test Case SPT-29 Device Seizure 5.0 build 4582.15907	
Analysis:	Expected results achieved

5.2.29 SPT-30 (iPhone4 GSM)

Test Case SPT-30 Device Seizure 5.0 build 4582.15907	
Case Summary:	SPT-30 After a successful SIM acquisition, alter the case file via third-party means and attempt to reopen the case.
Assertions:	SPT-AO-27 If the case file or individual data objects are modified via third-party means, then the tool shall provide protection mechanisms disallowing or reporting data modification.
Tester Name:	rpa
Test Host:	Morrisy
Test Date:	Fri Sep 21 14:45:09 EDT 2012
Device:	iPhone4 GSM
Source Setup:	OS: WIN XP v5.1.2600 Interface: USB
Log Highlights:	Created by Device Seizure v5.0 Acquisition started: Fri Sep 21 14:45:09 EDT 2012 Acquisition finished: Fri Sep 21 14:47:42 EDT 2012 Notification of modified SIM data was successful
Results:	

Assertion & Expected Result	Actual Result
SPT-AO-27 Notification of modified device case data.	as expected

Analysis:	Expected results achieved

5.2.30 SPT-33 (iPhone4 GSM)

Test Case SPT-33 Device Seizure 5.0 build 4582.15907	
Case Summary:	SPT-33 Acquire mobile device internal memory and review data containing non-ASCII characters.
Assertions:	SPT-AO-40 If the cellular forensic tool supports display of non-ASCII characters, then the application should present address book entries in their native format. SPT-AO-41 If the cellular forensic tool supports proper display of non-ASCII characters, then the application should present text messages in their native format.
Tester Name:	rpa
Test Host:	Morrisy
Test Date:	Fri Sep 21 14:48:35 EDT 2012
Device:	iPhone4 GSM
Source Setup:	OS: WIN XP v5.1.2600 Interface: cable
Log Highlights:	Created by Device Seizure v5.0 Acquisition started: Fri Sep 21 14:48:35 EDT 2012 Acquisition finished: Fri Sep 21 14:49:30 EDT 2012 Non-ASCII Address book entries were acquired and properly displayed Non-ASCII text messages were acquired and properly displayed
Results:	

Assertion & Expected Result	Actual Result
SPT-AO-40 Acquisition of non-ASCII address book entries/ADNs.	as expected
SPT-AO-41 Acquisition of non-ASCII text messages.	as expected

Test Case SPT-33 Device Seizure 5.0 build 4582.15907	
Analysis:	Expected results achieved

5.2.31 SPT-34 (iPhone4 GSM)

Test Case SPT-34 Device Seizure 5.0 build 4582.15907	
Case Summary:	SPT-34 Acquire SIM memory and review data containing non-ASCII characters.
Assertions:	SPT-AO-40 If the cellular forensic tool supports display of non-ASCII characters, then the application should present ADNs in their native format. SPT-AO-41 If the cellular forensic tool supports proper display of non-ASCII characters, then the application should present text messages in their native format.
Tester Name:	rpa
Test Host:	Morrisy
Test Date:	Fri Sep 21 14:48:52 EDT 2012
Device:	iPhone4 GSM
Source Setup:	OS: WIN XP v5.1.2600 Interface: USB
Log Highlights:	Created by Device Seizure v5.0 Acquisition started: Fri Sep 21 14:48:52 EDT 2012 Acquisition finished: Fri Sep 21 14:49:43 EDT 2012 Non-ASCII ADNs were acquired and properly displayed Non-ASCII text messages were acquired and properly displayed

Results:		
	Assertion & Expected Result	**Actual Result**
	SPT-AO-40 Acquisition of non-ASCII address book entries/ADNs.	as expected
	SPT-AO-41 Acquisition of non-ASCII text messages.	as expected

Analysis:	Expected results achieved

5.2.32 SPT-35 (iPhone4 GSM)

Test Case SPT-35 Device Seizure 5.0 build 4582.15907	
Case Summary:	SPT-35 Begin acquisition on a PIN protected SIM to determine if the tool provides an accurate count of the remaining number of PIN attempts and if the PIN attempts are decremented when entering an incorrect value.
Assertions:	SPT-AO-29 If a cellular forensic tool provides the examiner with the remaining number of authentication attempts, then the application should provide an accurate count of the remaining PIN attempts.
Tester Name:	rpa
Test Host:	Morrisy
Test Date:	Fri Sep 21 14:50:19 EDT 2012
Device:	iPhone4 GSM
Source Setup:	OS: WIN XP v5.1.2600 Interface: USB
Log Highlights:	Created by Device Seizure v5.0 Acquisition started: Fri Sep 21 14:50:19 EDT 2012 Acquisition finished: Fri Sep 21 14:53:15 EDT 2012 The remaining number of PIN attempts were properly displayed

Results:	
	Assertion & Expected Result ... **Actual Result**

Test Case SPT-35 Device Seizure 5.0 build 4582.15907	
	SPT-AO-29 Display remaining number of PIN attempts.	as expected
Analysis:	Expected results achieved

5.2.33 SPT-36 (iPhone4 GSM)

Test Case SPT-36 Device Seizure 5.0 build 4582.15907	
Case Summary:	SPT-36 Begin acquisition on a SIM whose PIN attempts have been exhausted to determine if the tool provides an accurate count of the remaining number of PUK attempts and if the PUK attempts are decremented when entering an incorrect value.
Assertions:	SPT-AO-30 If a cellular forensic tool provides the examiner with the remaining number of PUK attempts, then the application should provide an accurate count of the remaining PUK attempts.
Tester Name:	rpa
Test Host:	Morrisy
Test Date:	Fri Sep 21 14:50:32 EDT 2012
Device:	iPhone4 GSM
Source Setup:	OS: WIN XP v5.1.2600 Interface: USB
Log Highlights:	Created by Device Seizure v5.0 Acquisition started: Fri Sep 21 14:50:32 EDT 2012 Acquisition finished: Fri Sep 21 14:53:30 EDT 2012 Remaining number of PUK attempts were properly displayed
Results:	

Assertion & Expected Result	Actual Result
SPT-AO-30 Display remaining number of PUK attempts.	as expected

Analysis:	Expected results achieved

5.2.34 SPT-38 (iPhone4 GSM)

Test Case SPT-38 Device Seizure 5.0 build 4582.15907	
Case Summary:	SPT-38 Acquire mobile device internal memory and review hash values for vendor supported data objects.
Assertions:	SPT-AO-43 If the cellular forensic tool supports hashing for individual data objects, then the tool shall present the user with a hash value for each supported data object.
Tester Name:	rpa
Test Host:	Morrisy
Test Date:	Fri Sep 21 14:53:59 EDT 2012
Device:	iPhone4 GSM
Source Setup:	OS: WIN XP v5.1.2600 Interface: cable
Log Highlights:	Created by Device Seizure v5.0 Acquisition started: Fri Sep 21 14:53:59 EDT 2012 Acquisition finished: Fri Sep 21 14:58:02 EDT 2012 Hash values were properly reported for individually acquired device data elements
Results:	

Assertion & Expected Result	Actual Result
SPT-AO-43 Acquire data, check known hash values for consistency.	as expected

Test Case SPT-38 Device Seizure 5.0 build 4582.15907	
Analysis:	Expected results achieved

5.2.35 SPT-39 (iPhone4 GSM)

Test Case SPT-39 Device Seizure 5.0 build 4582.15907	
Case Summary:	SPT-39 Acquire SIM memory and review hash values for vendor supported data objects.
Assertions:	SPT-AO-43 If the cellular forensic tool supports hashing for individual data objects, then the tool shall present the user with a hash value for each supported data object.
Tester Name:	rpa
Test Host:	Morrisy
Test Date:	Fri Sep 21 14:54:17 EDT 2012
Device:	iPhone4 GSM
Source Setup:	OS: WIN XP v5.1.2600 Interface: USB
Log Highlights:	Created by Device Seizure v5.0 Acquisition started: Fri Sep 21 14:54:17 EDT 2012 Acquisition finished: Fri Sep 21 14:58:14 EDT 2012 Hash values were properly reported for individually acquired SIM data elements

Results:		
	Assertion & Expected Result	**Actual Result**
	SPT-AO-43 Acquire data, check known hash values for consistency.	as expected

Analysis:	Expected results achieved

5.2.36 SPT-01 (BlackBerry Torch)

Test Case SPT-01 Device Seizure 5.0 build 4582.15907	
Case Summary:	SPT-01 Acquire mobile device internal memory over tool-supported interfaces (e.g., cable, Bluetooth, IrDA).
Assertions:	SPT-CA-01 If a cellular forensic tool provides support for connectivity of the target device, then the tool shall successfully recognize the target device via all vendor supported interfaces (e.g., cable, Bluetooth, IrDA). SPT-CA-04 If a cellular forensic tool completes acquisition of the target device without error, then the tool shall have the ability to present acquired data objects in a useable format via either a preview pane or generated report. SPT-CA-29 If a cellular forensic tool provides the user with an "Acquire All" device data objects acquisition option, then the tool shall complete the acquisition of all data objects without error. SPT-CA-30 If a cellular forensic tool provides the user with a "Select All" individual device data objects, then the tool shall complete the acquisition of all individually selected data objects without error. SPT-CA-31 If a cellular forensic tool provides the user with the ability to "Select Individual" device data objects for acquisition, then the tool shall acquire each exclusive data object without error. SPT-CA-32 If a cellular forensic tool completes two consecutive logical acquisitions of the target device without error, then the payload (data objects) on the mobile device shall remain consistent.
Tester Name:	rpa
Test Host:	Morrisy
Test Date:	Mon Sep 24 12:38:24 EDT 2012
Device:	BlackBerry Torch
Source	OS: WIN XP v5.1.2600

Test Case SPT-01 Device Seizure 5.0 build 4582.15907	
Setup:	Interface: cable
Log Highlights:	Created by Device Seizure v5.0 Acquisition started: Mon Sep 24 12:38:24 EDT 2012 Acquisition finished: Mon Sep 24 12:39:50 EDT 2012 Device connectivity was established via supported interface
Results:	

Assertion & Expected Result	Actual Result
SPT-CA-01 Device connectivity via supported interfaces.	as expected
SPT-CA-04 Readability and completeness of acquired data via supported reports.	as expected
SPT-CA-29 Acquire-All data objects acquisition.	as expected
SPT-CA-30 Select-All data objects acquisition.	as expected
SPT-CA-31 Select-Individual data objects acquisition.	as expected
SPT-CA-32 Perform back-to-back acquisitions, check device payload for modifications.	as expected

Analysis:	Expected results achieved

5.2.37 SPT-02 (BlackBerry Torch)

Test Case SPT-02 Device Seizure 5.0 build 4582.15907	
Case Summary:	SPT-02 Attempt internal memory acquisition of a nonsupported mobile device.
Assertions:	SPT-CA-02 If a cellular forensic tool attempts to connect to a nonsupported device, then the tool shall notify the user that the device is not supported.
Tester Name:	rpa
Test Host:	Morrisy
Test Date:	Mon Sep 24 12:58:44 EDT 2012
Device:	unsupported device
Source Setup:	OS: WIN XP v5.1.2600 Interface: cable
Log Highlights:	Created by Device Seizure v5.0 Acquisition started: Mon Sep 24 12:58:44 EDT 2012 Acquisition finished: Mon Sep 24 13:00:48 EDT 2012 Identification of nonsupported devices was successful
Results:	

Assertion & Expected Result	Actual Result
SPT-CA-02 Identification of nonsupported devices.	as expected

Analysis:	Expected results achieved

5.2.38 SPT-03 (BlackBerry Torch)

Test Case SPT-03 Device Seizure 5.0 build 4582.15907	
Case Summary:	SPT-03 Begin mobile device internal memory acquisition and interrupt connectivity by interface disengagement.
Assertions:	SPT-CA-03 If connectivity between the mobile device and cellular forensic tool is disrupted, then the tool shall notify the user that connectivity has been disrupted.
Tester Name:	rpa
Test Host:	Morrisy
Test Date:	Mon Sep 24 13:00:40 EDT 2012
Device:	BlackBerry Torch

Test Case SPT-03 Device Seizure 5.0 build 4582.15907	
Source Setup:	OS: WIN XP v5.1.2600 Interface: cable
Log Highlights:	Created by Device Seizure v5.0 Acquisition started: Mon Sep 24 13:00:40 EDT 2012 Acquisition finished: Mon Sep 24 13:01:00 EDT 2012 Device acquisition disruption notification was successful
Results:	

Assertion & Expected Result	Actual Result
SPT-CA-03 Notification of device acquisition disruption.	as expected

Analysis:	Expected results achieved

5.2.39 SPT-04 (BlackBerry Torch)

Test Case SPT-04 Device Seizure 5.0 build 4582.15907	
Case Summary:	SPT-04 Acquire mobile device internal memory and review reported data via the preview pane or generated reports for readability.
Assertions:	SPT-CA-04 If a cellular forensic tool completes acquisition of the target device without error, then the tool shall have the ability to present acquired data objects in a useable format via either a preview pane or generated report.
Tester Name:	rpa
Test Host:	Morrisy
Test Date:	Mon Sep 24 12:59:06 EDT 2012
Device:	BlackBerry_Torch
Source Setup:	OS: WIN XP v5.1.2600 Interface: cable
Log Highlights:	Created by Device Seizure v5.0 Acquisition started: Mon Sep 24 12:59:06 EDT 2012 Acquisition finished: Mon Sep 24 13:01:14 EDT 2012 Readability and completeness of acquired data was successful
Results:	

Assertion & Expected Result	Actual Result
SPT-CA-04 Readability and completeness of acquired data via supported reports.	as expected

Analysis:	Expected results achieved

5.2.40 SPT-05 (BlackBerry Torch)

Test Case SPT-05 Device Seizure 5.0 build 4582.15907	
Case Summary:	SPT-05 Acquire mobile device internal memory and review reported subscriber and equipment-related information (e.g., IMEI/MEID/ESN, MSISDN).
Assertions:	SPT-CA-05 If a cellular forensic tool completes acquisition of the target device without error, then subscriber related information shall be presented in a useable format. SPT-CA-06 If a cellular forensic tool completes acquisition of the target device without error, then equipment-related information shall be presented in a useable format.
Tester Name:	rpa
Test Host:	Morrisy
Test Date:	Mon Sep 24 12:59:33 EDT 2012
Device:	BlackBerry Torch
Source Setup:	OS: WIN XP v5.1.2600 Interface: cable

Test Case SPT-05 Device Seizure 5.0 build 4582.15907	
Log Highlights:	Created by Device Seizure v5.0 Acquisition started: Mon Sep 24 12:59:33 EDT 2012 Acquisition finished: Mon Sep 24 13:01:30 EDT 2012 Subscriber and Equipment-related data (i.e., MSISDN, IMEI) were acquired
Results:	

Assertion & Expected Result	Actual Result
SPT-CA-05 Acquisition of MSISDN, IMSI.	as expected
SPT-CA-06 Acquisition of IMEI/MEID/ESN.	as expected

Analysis:	Expected results achieved

5.2.41 SPT-06 (BlackBerry Torch)

Test Case SPT-06 Device Seizure 5.0 build 4582.15907	
Case Summary:	SPT-06 Acquire mobile device internal memory and review reported PIM-related data.
Assertions:	SPT-CA-07 If a cellular forensic tool completes acquisition of the target device without error, then address book entries shall be presented in a useable format. SPT-CA-08 If a cellular forensic tool completes acquisition of the target device without error, then maximum length address book entries shall be presented in a useable format. SPT-CA-09 If a cellular forensic tool completes acquisition of the target device without error, then address book entries containing special characters shall be presented in a useable format. SPT-CA-10 If a cellular forensic tool completes acquisition of the target device without error, then address book entries containing blank names shall be presented in a useable format. SPT-CA-11 If a cellular forensic tool completes acquisition of the target device without error, then email addresses associated with address book entries shall be presented in a useable format. SPT-CA-12 If a cellular forensic tool completes acquisition of the target device without error, then graphics associated with address book entries shall be presented in a useable format. SPT-CA-13 If a cellular forensic tool completes acquisition of the target device without error, then datebook, calendar, note entries shall be presented in a useable format. SPT-CA-14 If a cellular forensic tool completes acquisition of the target device without error, then maximum length datebook, calendar, note entries shall be presented in a useable format.
Tester Name:	rpa
Test Host:	Morrisy
Test Date:	Mon Sep 24 13:04:22 EDT 2012
Device:	BlackBerry Torch
Source Setup:	OS: WIN XP v5.1.2600 Interface: cable
Log Highlights:	Created by Device Seizure v5.0 Acquisition started: Mon Sep 24 13:04:22 EDT 2012 Acquisition finished: Mon Sep 24 13:07:21 EDT 2012 Regular Length Address Book entries were acquired Maximum Length Address Book entries were acquired Special Character Address Book entries were acquired Blank Name Address Book entries were acquired Email addresses within Address Book entries were acquired Embedded graphics within Address Book entries were not acquired ALL PIM-related data was acquired **Notes:** Graphics files associated with address book entries were not reported.
Results:	

Test Case SPT-06 Device Seizure 5.0 build 4582.15907		
	Assertion & Expected Result	**Actual Result**
	SPT-CA-07 Acquisition of address book entries.	as expected
	SPT-CA-08 Acquisition of maximum length address book entries.	as expected
	SPT-CA-09 Acquisition of address book entries containing special characters.	as expected
	SPT-CA-10 Acquisition of address book entries containing a blank name entry.	as expected
	SPT-CA-11 Acquisition of embedded email addresses within address book entries.	as expected
	SPT-CA-12 Acquisition of embedded graphics within address book entries.	Not as expected
	SPT-CA-13 Acquisition of PIM data (i.e., datebook/calendar, notes).	as expected
	SPT-CA-14 Acquisition of maximum length PIM data.	as expected
Analysis:	Expected results not achieved	

5.2.42 SPT-07 (BlackBerry Torch)

Test Case SPT-07 Device Seizure 5.0 build 4582.15907	
Case Summary:	SPT-07 Acquire mobile device internal memory and review reported call logs.
Assertions:	SPT-CA-15 If a cellular forensic tool completes acquisition of the target device without error, then call logs (incoming/outgoing/missed) shall be presented in a useable format. SPT-CA-16 If a cellular forensic tool completes acquisition of the target device without error, then the corresponding date/time stamps and the duration of the call for call logs shall be presented in a useable format.
Tester Name:	rpa
Test Host:	Morrisy
Test Date:	Mon Sep 24 13:27:57 EDT 2012
Device:	BlackBerry Torch
Source Setup:	OS: WIN XP v5.1.2600 Interface: cable
Log Highlights:	Created by Device Seizure v5.0 Acquisition started: Mon Sep 24 13:27:57 EDT 2012 Acquisition finished: Mon Sep 24 13:30:30 EDT 2012 All Call Logs (incoming, outgoing, missed) were acquired All Call Log date/time stamps data were correctly reported
Results:	

Assertion & Expected Result	Actual Result
SPT-CA-15 Acquisition of call logs.	as expected
SPT-CA-16 Acquisition of call log date/time stamps.	as expected

Analysis:	Expected results achieved

5.2.43 SPT-08 (BlackBerry Torch)

Test Case SPT-08 Device Seizure 5.0 build 4582.15907	
Case Summary:	SPT-08 Acquire mobile device internal memory and review reported text messages.
Assertions:	SPT-CA-17 If a cellular forensic tool completes acquisition of the target device without error, then ASCII text messages (i.e., SMS, EMS) shall be presented in a useable format. SPT-CA-18 If a cellular forensic tool completes acquisition of the target device without error, then the corresponding date/time stamps for text messages shall be presented in a useable format.

Test Case SPT-08 Device Seizure 5.0 build 4582.15907	
	SPT-CA-19 If a cellular forensic tool completes acquisition of the target device without error, then the corresponding status (i.e., read, unread) for text messages shall be presented in a useable format. SPT-CA-20 If a cellular forensic tool completes acquisition of the target device without error, then the corresponding sender / recipient phone numbers for text messages shall be presented in a useable format.
Tester Name:	rpa
Test Host:	Morrisy
Test Date:	Mon Sep 24 13:28:15 EDT 2012
Device:	BlackBerry Torch
Source Setup:	OS: WIN XP v5.1.2600 Interface: cable
Log Highlights:	Created by Device Seizure v5.0 Acquisition started: Mon Sep 24 13:28:15 EDT 2012 Acquisition finished: Mon Sep 24 13:30:44 EDT 2012 ALL text messages (SMS, EMS) were acquired Correct date/time stamps were reported for all text messages Correct status flags were reported for all text messages Sender and Recipient phone numbers associated with text messages were correctly reported

Results:		
	Assertion & Expected Result	**Actual Result**
	SPT-CA-17 Acquisition of text messages.	as expected
	SPT-CA-18 Acquisition of text message date/time stamps.	as expected
	SPT-CA-19 Acquisition of text message status flags.	as expected
	SPT-CA-20 Acquisition of sender/recipient phone number associated with text messages.	as expected

Analysis:	Expected results achieved

5.2.44 SPT-09 (BlackBerry Torch)

Test Case SPT-09 Device Seizure 5.0 build 4582.15907	
Case Summary:	SPT-09 Acquire mobile device internal memory and review reported MMS multi-media-related data (i.e., text, audio, graphics, video).
Assertions:	SPT-CA-21 If a cellular forensic tool completes acquisition of the target device without error, then MMS messages and associated audio shall be presented in a useable format. SPT-CA-22 If a cellular forensic tool completes acquisition of the target device without error, then MMS messages and associated graphic files shall be presented in a useable format. SPT-CA-23 If a cellular forensic tool completes acquisition of the target device without error, then MMS messages and associated video shall be presented in a useable format.
Tester Name:	rpa
Test Host:	Morrisy
Test Date:	Mon Sep 24 13:38:57 EDT 2012
Device:	BlackBerry Torch
Source Setup:	OS: WIN XP v5.1.2600 Interface: cable
Log Highlights:	Created by Device Seizure v5.0 Acquisition started: Mon Sep 24 13:38:57 EDT 2012 Acquisition finished: Mon Sep 24 13:43:26 EDT 2012 Partial audio MMS messages were acquired Partial image MMS messages were acquired Partial video MMS messages were acquired **Notes:**

	Acquisition of attached audio, graphics, and video were not reported.

Results:		
	Assertion & Expected Result	**Actual Result**
	SPT-CA-21 Acquisition of audio MMS messages.	Not as expected
	SPT-CA-22 Acquisition of graphic data image MMS messages.	Not as expected
	SPT-CA-23 Acquisition of video MMS messages.	Not as expected

Analysis:	Partial results achieved

5.2.45 SPT-10 (BlackBerry Torch)

Case Summary:	SPT-10 Acquire mobile device internal memory and review reported stand-alone multi-media data (i.e., audio, graphics, video).
Assertions:	SPT-CA-24 If a cellular forensic tool completes acquisition of the target device without error, then stand-alone audio files shall be presented in a useable format via either an internal application or suggested third-party application. SPT-CA-25 If a cellular forensic tool completes acquisition of the target device without error, then stand-alone graphic files shall be presented in a useable format via either an internal application or suggested third-party application. SPT-CA-26 If a cellular forensic tool completes acquisition of the target device without error, then stand-alone video files shall be presented in a useable format via either an internal application or suggested third-party application.
Tester Name:	rpa
Test Host:	Morrisy
Test Date:	Mon Sep 24 13:31:25 EDT 2012
Device:	BlackBerry Torch
Source Setup:	OS: WIN XP v5.1.2600 Interface: cable
Log Highlights:	Created by Device Seizure v5.0 Acquisition started: Mon Sep 24 13:31:25 EDT 2012 Acquisition finished: Mon Sep 24 13:33:14 EDT 2012 Audio files were not acquired Image files were not acquired Video files were not acquired

Results:		
	Assertion & Expected Result	**Actual Result**
	SPT-CA-24 Acquisition of stand-alone audio files.	as expected
	SPT-CA-25 Acquisition of stand-alone graphic files.	as expected
	SPT-CA-26 Acquisition of stand-alone video files.	as expected

Analysis:	Expected results achieved

5.2.46 SPT-12 (BlackBerry Torch)

Case Summary:	SPT-12 Acquire mobile device internal memory and review Internet-related data (i.e., bookmarks, visited sites.
Assertions:	SPT-CA-28 If a cellular forensic tool completes acquisition of the target device without error, then Internet-related data (i.e., bookmarks, visited sites) cached to the device shall be acquired and presented in a useable

Test Case SPT-12 Device Seizure 5.0 build 4582.15907	
	format.
Tester Name:	rpa
Test Host:	Morrisy
Test Date:	Mon Sep 24 13:49:17 EDT 2012
Device:	BlackBerry_Torch
Source Setup:	OS: WIN XP v5.1.2600 Interface: cable
Log Highlights:	Created by Device Seizure v5.0 Acquisition started: Mon Sep 24 13:49:17 EDT 2012 Acquisition finished: Mon Sep 24 13:51:53 EDT 2012 All Internet-related data was acquired
Results:	

Assertion & Expected Result	Actual Result
SPT-CA-28 Acquisition of Internet-related data.	as expected

Analysis:	Expected results achieved

5.2.47 SPT-13 (BlackBerry Torch)

Test Case SPT-13 Device Seizure 5.0 build 4582.15907	
Case Summary:	SPT-13 Acquire mobile device internal memory by selecting a combination of supported data elements.
Assertions:	SPT-CA-29 If a cellular forensic tool provides the user with an "Acquire All" device data objects acquisition option, then the tool shall complete the acquisition of all data objects without error. SPT-CA-30 If a cellular forensic tool provides the user with an "Select All" individual device data objects, then the tool shall complete the acquisition of all individually selected data objects without error. SPT-CA-31 If a cellular forensic tool provides the user with the ability to "Select Individual" device data objects for acquisition, then the tool shall acquire each exclusive data object without error.
Tester Name:	rpa
Test Host:	Morrisy
Test Date:	Mon Sep 24 12:38:53 EDT 2012
Device:	BlackBerry Torch
Source Setup:	OS: WIN XP v5.1.2600 Interface: cable
Log Highlights:	Created by Device Seizure v5.0 Acquisition started: Mon Sep 24 12:38:53 EDT 2012 Acquisition finished: Mon Sep 24 12:40:03 EDT 2012 Acquire All acquisition was successful
Results:	

Assertion & Expected Result	Actual Result
SPT-CA-29 Acquire-All data objects acquisition.	as expected
SPT-CA-30 Select-All data objects acquisition.	as expected
SPT-CA-31 Select-Individual data objects acquisition.	as expected

Analysis:	Expected results achieved

5.2.48 SPT-14 (BlackBerry Torch)

Test Case SPT-14 Device Seizure 5.0 build 4582.15907	
Case Summary:	SPT-14 Acquire SIM memory over supported interfaces (e.g., PC/SC reader).
Assertions:	SPT-AO-01 If a cellular forensic tool provides support for connectivity of

Test Case SPT-14 Device Seizure 5.0 build 4582.15907	
	the target SIM, then the tool shall successfully recognize the target SIM via all tool-supported interfaces (e.g., PC/SC reader, proprietary reader, Smart Phone itself).
Tester Name:	rpa
Test Host:	Morrisy
Test Date:	Mon Sep 24 08:21:23 EDT 2012
Device:	BlackBerry_Torch
Source Setup:	OS: WIN XP v5.1.2600 Interface: USB
Log Highlights:	Created by Device Seizure v5.0 Acquisition started: Mon Sep 24 08:21:23 EDT 2012 Acquisition finished: Mon Sep 24 08:26:18 EDT 2012 Media connectivity was established via supported interface
Results:	

Assertion & Expected Result	Actual Result
SPT-AO-01 SIM connectivity via supported interfaces.	as expected

Analysis:	Expected results achieved

5.2.49 SPT-15 (BlackBerry Torch)

Test Case SPT-15 Device Seizure 5.0 build 4582.15907	
Case Summary:	SPT-15 Attempt acquisition of a nonsupported SIM.
Assertions:	SPT-AO-02 If a cellular forensic tool attempts to connect to a nonsupported SIM, then the tool shall notify the user that the SIM is not supported.
Tester Name:	rpa
Test Host:	Morrisy
Test Date:	Mon Sep 24 08:22:28 EDT 2012
Device:	BlackBerry_Torch
Source Setup:	OS: WIN XP v5.1.2600 Interface: USB
Log Highlights:	Created by Device Seizure v5.0 Acquisition started: Mon Sep 24 08:22:28 EDT 2012 Acquisition finished: Mon Sep 24 08:26:34 EDT 2012 Identification of nonsupported media was successful
Results:	

Assertion & Expected Result	Actual Result
SPT-AO-02 Identification of nonsupported SIMs.	as expected

Analysis:	Expected results achieved

5.2.50 SPT-16 (BlackBerry Torch)

Test Case SPT-16 Device Seizure 5.0 build 4582.15907	
Case Summary:	SPT-16 Begin SIM acquisition and interrupt connectivity by interface disengagement.
Assertions:	SPT-AO-03 If a cellular forensic tool loses connectivity with the SIM reader, then the tool shall notify the user that connectivity has been disrupted.
Tester Name:	rpa
Test Host:	Morrisy
Test Date:	Mon Sep 24 08:22:57 EDT 2012

Test Case SPT-16 Device Seizure 5.0 build 4582.15907	
Device:	BlackBerry Torch
Source Setup:	OS: WIN XP v5.1.2600 Interface: USB
Log Highlights:	Created by Device Seizure v5.0 Acquisition started: Mon Sep 24 08:22:57 EDT 2012 Acquisition finished: Mon Sep 24 08:26:47 EDT 2012 Media acquisition disruption notification was successful
Results:	

Assertion & Expected Result	Actual Result
SPT-AO-03 Notification of SIM acquisition disruption.	as expected

Analysis:	Expected results achieved

5.2.51 SPT-18 (BlackBerry Torch)

Test Case SPT-18 Device Seizure 5.0 build 4582.15907	
Case Summary:	SPT-18 Acquire SIM memory and review reported Abbreviated Dialing Numbers (ADN).
Assertions:	SPT-AO-08 If a cellular forensic tool completes acquisition of the target SIM without error, then ASCII Abbreviated Dialing Numbers (ADN) shall be presented in a useable format. SPT-AO-09 If a cellular forensic tool completes acquisition of the target SIM without error, then maximum length ADNs shall be presented in a useable format. SPT-AO-10 If a cellular forensic tool completes acquisition of the SIM without error, then ADNs containing special characters shall be presented in a useable format. SPT-AO-11 If a cellular forensic tool completes acquisition of the SIM without error, then ADNs containing blank names shall be presented in a useable format.
Tester Name:	rpa
Test Host:	Morrisy
Test Date:	Mon Sep 24 08:23:50 EDT 2012
Device:	BlackBerry Torch
Source Setup:	OS: WIN XP v5.1.2600 Interface: USB
Log Highlights:	Created by Device Seizure v5.0 Acquisition started: Mon Sep 24 08:23:50 EDT 2012 Acquisition finished: Mon Sep 24 08:27:54 EDT 2012 All ADNs were acquired
Results:	

Assertion & Expected Result	Actual Result
SPT-AO-08 Acquisition of ADNs.	as expected
SPT-AO-09 Acquisition of maximum length ADNs.	as expected
SPT-AO-10 Acquisition of special character ADNs.	as expected
SPT-AO-11 Acquisition of blank name ADNs.	as expected

Analysis:	Expected results achieved

5.2.52 SPT-19 (BlackBerry Torch)

Test Case SPT-19 Device Seizure 5.0 build 4582.15907	
Case Summary:	SPT-19 Acquire SIM memory and review reported Last Numbers Dialed (LND).
Assertions:	SPT-AO-12 If a cellular forensic tool completes acquisition of the target SIM without error, then Last Numbers Dialed (LND) shall be presented in a useable format. SPT-AO-13 If a cellular forensic tool completes acquisition of the target

Test Case SPT-19 Device Seizure 5.0 build 4582.15907	
	SIM without error, then the corresponding date/time stamps for LNDs shall be presented in a useable format.
Tester Name:	rpa
Test Host:	Morrisy
Test Date:	Mon Sep 24 08:24:21 EDT 2012
Device:	BlackBerry Torch
Source Setup:	OS: WIN XP v5.1.2600 Interface: USB
Log Highlights:	Created by Device Seizure v5.0 Acquisition started: Mon Sep 24 08:24:21 EDT 2012 Acquisition finished: Mon Sep 24 08:28:08 EDT 2012 LNDs were acquired Date/Time Stamps correctly reported for LNDs
Results:	

Assertion & Expected Result	Actual Result
SPT-AO-12 Acquisition of LNDs.	as expected
SPT-AO-13 Acquisition of LND date/time stamps.	as expected

Analysis:	Expected results achieved

5.2.53 SPT-20 (BlackBerry Torch)

Test Case SPT-20 Device Seizure 5.0 build 4582.15907	
Case Summary:	SPT-20 Acquire SIM memory and review reported text messages (SMS, EMS).
Assertions:	SPT-AO-14 If a cellular forensic tool completes acquisition of the target SIM without error, then ASCII SMS text messages shall be presented in a useable format. SPT-AO-15 If a cellular forensic tool completes acquisition of the target SIM without error, then ASCII EMS text messages shall be presented in a useable format. SPT-AO-16 If a cellular forensic tool completes acquisition of the target SIM without error, then the corresponding date/time stamps for all text messages shall be presented in a useable format. SPT-AO-17 If a cellular forensic tool completes acquisition of the target SIM without error, then the corresponding status (i.e., read, unread) for text messages shall be presented in a useable format. SPT-AO-18 If a cellular forensic tool completes acquisition of the target SIM without error, then the corresponding sender / recipient phone numbers for text messages shall be presented in a useable format.
Tester Name:	rpa
Test Host:	Morrisy
Test Date:	Mon Sep 24 08:30:15 EDT 2012
Device:	BlackBerry Torch
Source Setup:	OS: WIN XP v5.1.2600 Interface: USB
Log Highlights:	Created by Device Seizure v5.0 Acquisition started: Mon Sep 24 08:30:15 EDT 2012 Acquisition finished: Mon Sep 24 08:34:32 EDT 2012 ALL text messages (SMS, EMS) were acquired All date/time stamps were reported for text messages Correct status flags were reported for text messages Sender and Recipient phone numbers associated with text messages were correctly reported
Results:	

Assertion & Expected Result	Actual Result
SPT-AO-14 Acquisition of SMS messages.	as expected

Test Case SPT-20 Device Seizure 5.0 build 4582.15907		
	SPT-AO-15 Acquisition of EMS messages.	as expected
	SPT-AO-16 Acquisition of text message date/time stamps.	as expected
	SPT-AO-17 Acquisition of text message status flags.	as expected
	SPT-AO-18 Acquisition of sender/recipient phone number associated with text messages.	as expected
Analysis:	Expected results achieved	

5.2.54 SPT-21 (BlackBerry Torch)

Test Case SPT-21 Device Seizure 5.0 build 4582.15907	
Case Summary:	SPT-21 Acquire SIM memory and review recoverable deleted text messages (SMS, EMS).
Assertions:	SPT-AO-19 If the cellular forensic tool completes acquisition of the target SIM without error, then deleted text messages that have not been overwritten shall be presented in a useable format.
Tester Name:	rpa
Test Host:	Morrisy
Test Date:	Mon Sep 24 08:30:41 EDT 2012
Device:	BlackBerry Torch
Source Setup:	OS: WIN XP v5.1.2600 Interface: USB
Log Highlights:	Created by Device Seizure v5.0 Acquisition started: Mon Sep 24 08:30:41 EDT 2012 Acquisition finished: Mon Sep 24 08:35:03 EDT 2012 Deleted text message data was recovered

Results:		
	Assertion & Expected Result	**Actual Result**
	SPT-AO-19 Acquisition of non-overwritten deleted text messages.	as expected

Analysis:	Expected results achieved

5.2.55 SPT-22 (BlackBerry Torch)

Test Case SPT-22 Device Seizure 5.0 build 4582.15907	
Case Summary:	SPT-22 Acquire SIM memory and review reported location-related data (i.e., LOCI, GPRSLOCI).
Assertions:	SPT-AO-20 If a cellular forensic tool completes acquisition of the target SIM without error, then location-related data (i.e., LOCI) shall be presented in a useable format. SPT-AO-21 If a cellular forensic tool completes acquisition of the target SIM without error, then location-related data (i.e., GRPSLOCI) shall be presented in a useable format.
Tester Name:	rpa
Test Host:	Morrisy
Test Date:	Mon Sep 24 08:31:01 EDT 2012
Device:	BlackBerry Torch
Source Setup:	OS: WIN XP v5.1.2600 Interface: USB
Log Highlights:	Created by Device Seizure v5.0 Acquisition started: Mon Sep 24 08:31:01 EDT 2012 Acquisition finished: Mon Sep 24 08:35:21 EDT 2012 LOCI data was acquired GPRSLOCI data was acquired

Test Case SPT-22 Device Seizure 5.0 build 4582.15907	
Results:	

Assertion & Expected Result	Actual Result
SPT-AO-20 Acquisition of LOCI information.	as expected
SPT-AO-21 Acquisition of GPRSLOCI information.	as expected

Analysis:	Expected results achieved

5.2.56 SPT-23 (BlackBerry Torch)

Test Case SPT-23 Device Seizure 5.0 build 4582.15907	
Case Summary:	SPT-23 Acquire SIM memory by selecting a combination of supported data elements.
Assertions:	SPT-AO-01 If a cellular forensic tool provides support for connectivity of the target SIM, then the tool shall successfully recognize the target SIM via all tool-supported interfaces (e.g., PC/SC reader, proprietary reader, Smart Phone itself). SPT-AO-22 If a cellular forensic tool provides the user with an "Acquire All" SIM data objects acquisition option, then the tool shall complete the acquisition of all data objects without error. SPT-AO-23 If a cellular forensic tool provides the user with an "Select All" individual SIM data objects, then the tool shall complete the acquisition of all individually selected data objects without error. SPT-AO-24 If a cellular forensic tool provides the user with the ability to "Select Individual" SIM data objects for acquisition, then the tool shall acquire each exclusive data object without error.
Tester Name:	rpa
Test Host:	Morrisy
Test Date:	Mon Sep 24 08:31:23 EDT 2012
Device:	BlackBerry Torch
Source Setup:	OS: WIN XP v5.1.2600 Interface: USB
Log Highlights:	Created by Device Seizure v5.0 Acquisition started: Mon Sep 24 08:31:23 EDT 2012 Acquisition finished: Mon Sep 24 08:35:36 EDT 2012 Acquire All acquisition was successful
Results:	

Assertion & Expected Result	Actual Result
SPT-AO-01 SIM connectivity via supported interfaces.	as expected
SPT-AO-22 Acquire-All data objects acquisition.	as expected
SPT-AO-23 Select-All data objects acquisition.	as expected
SPT-AO-24 Select-Individual data objects acquisition.	as expected

Analysis:	Expected results achieved

5.2.57 SPT-24 (BlackBerry Torch)

Test Case SPT-24 Device Seizure 5.0 build 4582.15907	
Case Summary:	SPT-24 Acquire mobile device internal memory and review reported data via supported generated report formats.
Assertions:	SPT-AO-25 If a cellular forensic tool completes acquisition of the target device without error, then the tool shall present the acquired data in a useable format via supported generated report formats.
Tester Name:	rpa
Test Host:	Morrisy
Test Date:	Mon Sep 24 13:59:01 EDT 2012
Device:	BlackBerry Torch

Test Case SPT-24 Device Seizure 5.0 build 4582.15907	
Source Setup:	OS: WIN XP v5.1.2600 Interface: cable
Log Highlights:	Created by Device Seizure v5.0 Acquisition started: Mon Sep 24 13:59:01 EDT 2012 Acquisition finished: Mon Sep 24 14:00:45 EDT 2012 Complete representation of known data via generated reports was successful
Results:	

Assertion & Expected Result	Actual Result
SPT-AO-25 Comparison of known device data elements via generated reports.	as expected

Analysis:	Expected results achieved

5.2.58 SPT-25 (BlackBerry Torch)

Test Case SPT-25 Device Seizure 5.0 build 4582.15907	
Case Summary:	SPT-25 Acquire mobile device internal memory and review reported data via the preview pane.
Assertions:	SPT-AO-26 If a cellular forensic tool completes acquisition of the target device without error, then the tool shall present the acquired data in a useable format in a preview pane view.
Tester Name:	rpa
Test Host:	Morrisy
Test Date:	Mon Sep 24 13:59:21 EDT 2012
Device:	BlackBerry_Torch
Source Setup:	OS: WIN XP v5.1.2600 Interface: cable
Log Highlights:	Created by Device Seizure v5.0 Acquisition started: Mon Sep 24 13:59:21 EDT 2012 Acquisition finished: Mon Sep 24 14:01:03 EDT 2012 Complete representation of known data via preview pane was successful
Results:	

Assertion & Expected Result	Actual Result
SPT-AO-26 Comparison of known device data elements via preview pane.	as expected

Analysis:	Expected results achieved

5.2.59 SPT-26 (BlackBerry Torch)

Test Case SPT-26 Device Seizure 5.0 build 4582.15907	
Case Summary:	SPT-26 Acquire SIM memory and review reported data via supported generated report formats.
Assertions:	SPT-AO-25 If a cellular forensic tool completes acquisition of the SIM without error, then the tool shall present the acquired data in a useable format via supported generated report formats.
Tester Name:	rpa
Test Host:	Morrisy
Test Date:	Mon Sep 24 08:32:41 EDT 2012
Device:	BlackBerry_Torch
Source Setup:	OS: WIN XP v5.1.2600 Interface: USB
Log	Created by Device Seizure v5.0

Test Case SPT-26 Device Seizure 5.0 build 4582.15907	
Highlights:	Acquisition started: Mon Sep 24 08:32:41 EDT 2012 Acquisition finished: Mon Sep 24 08:36:27 EDT 2012 Complete representation of known data via generated reports was successful
Results:	

Assertion & Expected Result	Actual Result
SPT-AO-25 Comparison of known device data elements via generated reports.	as expected

Analysis:	Expected results achieved

5.2.60 SPT-27 (BlackBerry Torch)

Test Case SPT-27 Device Seizure 5.0 build 4582.15907	
Case Summary:	SPT-27 Acquire SIM memory and review reported data via the preview pane.
Assertions:	SPT-AO-26 If a cellular forensic tool completes acquisition of the SIM without error, then the tool shall present the acquired data in a useable format in a preview pane view.
Tester Name:	rpa
Test Host:	Morrisy
Test Date:	Mon Sep 24 08:33:14 EDT 2012
Device:	BlackBerry Torch
Source Setup:	OS: WIN XP v5.1.2600 Interface: USB
Log Highlights:	Created by Device Seizure v5.0 Acquisition started: Mon Sep 24 08:33:14 EDT 2012 Acquisition finished: Mon Sep 24 08:36:41 EDT 2012 Complete representation of known data via preview pane was successful
Results:	

Assertion & Expected Result	Actual Result
SPT-AO-26 Comparison of known device data elements via preview pane.	as expected

Analysis:	Expected results achieved

5.2.61 SPT-28 (BlackBerry Torch)

Test Case SPT-28 Device Seizure 5.0 build 4582.15907	
Case Summary:	SPT-28 Attempt acquisition of a password-protected SIM.
Assertions:	SPT-AO-28 If the SIM is password-protected, then the cellular forensic tool shall provide the examiner with the opportunity to input the PIN before acquisition.
Tester Name:	rpa
Test Host:	Morrisy
Test Date:	Mon Sep 24 08:33:40 EDT 2012
Device:	BlackBerry Torch
Source Setup:	OS: WIN XP v5.1.2600 Interface: USB
Log Highlights:	Created by Device Seizure v5.0 Acquisition started: Mon Sep 24 08:33:40 EDT 2012 Acquisition finished: Mon Sep 24 08:36:57 EDT 2012

Test Case SPT-28 Device Seizure 5.0 build 4582.15907	
	Ability to enter PIN on protected media before acquisition was successful
Results:	
	Assertion & Expected Result | **Actual Result** SPT-AO-28 Acquisition of password protected SIM. | as expected
Analysis:	Expected results achieved

5.2.62 SPT-29 (BlackBerry Torch)

Test Case SPT-29 Device Seizure 5.0 build 4582.15907	
Case Summary:	SPT-29 After a successful mobile device internal memory, alter the case file via third-party means and attempt to reopen the case.
Assertions:	SPT-AO-27 If the case file or individual data objects are modified via third-party means, then the tool shall provide protection mechanisms disallowing or reporting data modification.
Tester Name:	rpa
Test Host:	Morrisy
Test Date:	Mon Sep 24 14:01:41 EDT 2012
Device:	BlackBerry Torch
Source Setup:	OS: WIN XP v5.1.2600 Interface: cable
Log Highlights:	Created by Device Seizure v5.0 Acquisition started: Mon Sep 24 14:01:41 EDT 2012 Acquisition finished: Mon Sep 24 14:02:52 EDT 2012 Notification of modified device memory data was successful
Results:	
	Assertion & Expected Result | **Actual Result** SPT-AO-27 Notification of modified device case data. | as expected
Analysis:	Expected results achieved

5.2.63 SPT-30 (BlackBerry Torch)

Test Case SPT-30 Device Seizure 5.0 build 4582.15907	
Case Summary:	SPT-30 After a successful SIM acquisition, alter the case file via third-party means and attempt to reopen the case.
Assertions:	SPT-AO-27 If the case file or individual data objects are modified via third-party means, then the tool shall provide protection mechanisms disallowing or reporting data modification.
Tester Name:	rpa
Test Host:	Morrisy
Test Date:	Mon Sep 24 08:42:17 EDT 2012
Device:	BlackBerry Torch
Source Setup:	OS: WIN XP v5.1.2600 Interface: USB
Log Highlights:	Created by Device Seizure v5.0 Acquisition started: Mon Sep 24 08:42:17 EDT 2012 Acquisition finished: Mon Sep 24 08:55:37 EDT 2012 Notification of modified SIM data was successful
Results:	
	Assertion & Expected Result | **Actual Result** SPT-AO-27 Notification of modified device case data. | as expected

Test Case SPT-30 Device Seizure 5.0 build 4582.15907	
Analysis:	Expected results achieved

5.2.64 SPT-33 (BlackBerry Torch)

Test Case SPT-33 Device Seizure 5.0 build 4582.15907	
Case Summary:	SPT-33 Acquire mobile device internal memory and review data containing non-ASCII characters.
Assertions:	SPT-AO-40 If the cellular forensic tool supports display of non-ASCII characters, then the application should present address book entries in their native format. SPT-AO-41 If the cellular forensic tool supports proper display of non-ASCII characters, then the application should present text messages in their native format.
Tester Name:	rpa
Test Host:	Morrisy
Test Date:	Mon Sep 24 14:03:35 EDT 2012
Device:	BlackBerry Torch
Source Setup:	OS: WIN XP v5.1.2600 Interface: cable
Log Highlights:	Created by Device Seizure v5.0 Acquisition started: Mon Sep 24 14:03:35 EDT 2012 Acquisition finished: Mon Sep 24 14:10:19 EDT 2012 Non-ASCII Address book entries were not acquired Non-ASCII text messages were acquired and properly displayed **Notes:** Contact entries made up of Chinese characters were not reported. Text messages containing the charactere é was reported as |
Results:	

Assertion & Expected Result	Actual Result
SPT-AO-40 Acquisition of non-ASCII address book entries/ADNs.	Not as expected
SPT-AO-41 Acquisition of non-ASCII text messages.	Not as expected

Analysis:	Expected results not achieved

5.2.65 SPT-34 (BlackBerry Torch)

Test Case SPT-34 Device Seizure 5.0 build 4582.15907	
Case Summary:	SPT-34 Acquire SIM memory and review data containing non-ASCII characters.
Assertions:	SPT-AO-40 If the cellular forensic tool supports display of non-ASCII characters, then the application should present ADNs in their native format. SPT-AO-41 If the cellular forensic tool supports proper display of non-ASCII characters, then the application should present text messages in their native format.
Tester Name:	rpa
Test Host:	Morrisy
Test Date:	Mon Sep 24 08:42:47 EDT 2012
Device:	BlackBerry Torch
Source Setup:	OS: WIN XP v5.1.2600 Interface: USB
Log Highlights:	Created by Device Seizure v5.0 Acquisition started: Mon Sep 24 08:42:47 EDT 2012 Acquisition finished: Mon Sep 24 08:56:03 EDT 2012

Test Case SPT-34 Device Seizure 5.0 build 4582.15907	
	Non-ASCII ADNs were acquired and properly displayed Non-ASCII text messages were acquired and properly displayed
Results:	

Assertion & Expected Result	Actual Result
SPT-AO-40 Acquisition of non-ASCII address book entries/ADNs.	as expected
SPT-AO-41 Acquisition of non-ASCII text messages.	as expected

Analysis:	Expected results achieved

5.2.66 SPT-35 (BlackBerry Torch)

Test Case SPT-35 Device Seizure 5.0 build 4582.15907	
Case Summary:	SPT-35 Begin acquisition on a PIN protected SIM to determine if the tool provides an accurate count of the remaining number of PIN attempts and if the PIN attempts are decremented when entering an incorrect value.
Assertions:	SPT-AO-29 If a cellular forensic tool provides the examiner with the remaining number of authentication attempts, then the application should provide an accurate count of the remaining PIN attempts.
Tester Name:	rpa
Test Host:	Morrisy
Test Date:	Mon Sep 24 08:53:13 EDT 2012
Device:	BlackBerry_Torch
Source Setup:	OS: WIN XP v5.1.2600 Interface: USB
Log Highlights:	Created by Device Seizure v5.0 Acquisition started: Mon Sep 24 08:53:13 EDT 2012 Acquisition finished: Mon Sep 24 08:56:29 EDT 2012 The remaining number of PIN attempts were properly displayed
Results:	

Assertion & Expected Result	Actual Result
SPT-AO-29 Display remaining number of PIN attempts.	as expected

Analysis:	Expected results achieved

5.2.67 SPT-36 (BlackBerry Torch)

Test Case SPT-36 Device Seizure 5.0 build 4582.15907	
Case Summary:	SPT-36 Begin acquisition on a SIM whose PIN attempts have been exhausted to determine if the tool provides an accurate count of the remaining number of PUK attempts and if the PUK attempts are decremented when entering an incorrect value.
Assertions:	SPT-AO-30 If a cellular forensic tool provides the examiner with the remaining number of PUK attempts, then the application should provide an accurate count of the remaining PUK attempts.
Tester Name:	rpa
Test Host:	Morrisy
Test Date:	Mon Sep 24 08:53:37 EDT 2012
Device:	BlackBerry Torch
Source Setup:	OS: WIN XP v5.1.2600 Interface: USB
Log Highlights:	Created by Device Seizure v5.0 Acquisition started: Mon Sep 24 08:53:37 EDT 2012 Acquisition finished: Mon Sep 24 08:56:50 EDT 2012

Test Case SPT-36 Device Seizure 5.0 build 4582.15907		
	Remaining number of PUK attempts were properly displayed	
Results:		
	Assertion & Expected Result	**Actual Result**
	SPT-AO-30 Display remaining number of PUK attempts.	as expected
Analysis:	Expected results achieved	

5.2.68 SPT-38 (BlackBerry Torch)

Test Case SPT-38 Device Seizure 5.0 build 4582.15907		
Case Summary:	SPT-38 Acquire mobile device internal memory and review hash values for vendor supported data objects.	
Assertions:	SPT-AO-43 If the cellular forensic tool supports hashing for individual data objects, then the tool shall present the user with a hash value for each supported data object.	
Tester Name:	rpa	
Test Host:	Morrisy	
Test Date:	Mon Sep 24 14:16:06 EDT 2012	
Device:	BlackBerry_Torch	
Source Setup:	OS: WIN XP v5.1.2600 Interface: cable	
Log Highlights:	Created by Device Seizure v5.0 Acquisition started: Mon Sep 24 14:16:06 EDT 2012 Acquisition finished: Mon Sep 24 14:18:14 EDT 2012 Hash values were properly reported for individually acquired device data elements	
Results:		
	Assertion & Expected Result	**Actual Result**
	SPT-AO-43 Acquire data, check known hash values for consistency.	as expected
Analysis:	Expected results achieved	

5.2.69 SPT-39 (BlackBerry Torch)

Test Case SPT-39 Device Seizure 5.0 build 4582.15907		
Case Summary:	SPT-39 Acquire SIM memory and review hash values for vendor supported data objects.	
Assertions:	SPT-AO-43 If the cellular forensic tool supports hashing for individual data objects, then the tool shall present the user with a hash value for each supported data object.	
Tester Name:	rpa	
Test Host:	Morrisy	
Test Date:	Mon Sep 24 08:54:07 EDT 2012	
Device:	BlackBerry Torch	
Source Setup:	OS: WIN XP v5.1.2600 Interface: USB	
Log Highlights:	Created by Device Seizure v5.0 Acquisition started: Mon Sep 24 08:54:07 EDT 2012 Acquisition finished: Mon Sep 24 08:57:24 EDT 2012 Hash values were properly reported for individually acquired SIM data elements	

Test Case SPT-39 Device Seizure 5.0 build 4582.15907		
Results:		
	Assertion & Expected Result	**Actual Result**
	SPT-AO-43 Acquire data, check known hash values for consistency.	as expected
Analysis:	Expected results achieved	

5.2.70 SPT-01 (Nokia 6350)

Test Case SPT-01 Device Seizure 5.0 build 4582.15907		
Case Summary:	SPT-01 Acquire mobile device internal memory over tool-supported interfaces (e.g., cable, Bluetooth, IrDA).	
Assertions:	SPT-CA-01 If a cellular forensic tool provides support for connectivity of the target device, then the tool shall successfully recognize the target device via all vendor supported interfaces (e.g., cable, Bluetooth, IrDA). SPT-CA-04 If a cellular forensic tool completes acquisition of the target device without error, then the tool shall have the ability to present acquired data objects in a useable format via either a preview pane or generated report. SPT-CA-29 If a cellular forensic tool provides the user with an "Acquire All" device data objects acquisition option, then the tool shall complete the acquisition of all data objects without error. SPT-CA-30 If a cellular forensic tool provides the user with a "Select All" individual device data objects, then the tool shall complete the acquisition of all individually selected data objects without error. SPT-CA-31 If a cellular forensic tool provides the user with the ability to "Select Individual" device data objects for acquisition, then the tool shall acquire each exclusive data object without error. SPT-CA-32 If a cellular forensic tool completes two consecutive logical acquisitions of the target device without error, then the payload (data objects) on the mobile device shall remain consistent.	
Tester Name:	rpa	
Test Host:	Morrisy	
Test Date:	Mon Sep 24 07:11:00 EDT 2012	
Device:	Nokia6350	
Source Setup:	OS: WIN XP v5.1.2600 Interface: cable	
Log Highlights:	Created by Device Seizure v5.0 Acquisition started: Mon Sep 24 07:11:00 EDT 2012 Acquisition finished: Mon Sep 24 07:12:34 EDT 2012 Device Connectivity was not established via supported interface **Notes:** The following error message was reported after attempting connectivity: Acquisition process has failed Result: Connection Error	
Results:		
	Assertion & Expected Result	**Actual Result**
	SPT-CA-01 Device connectivity via supported interfaces.	Not as expected
	SPT-CA-04 Readability and completeness of acquired data via supported reports.	NA
	SPT-CA-29 Acquire-All data objects acquisition.	NA
	SPT-CA-30 Select-All data objects acquisition.	NA
	SPT-CA-31 Select-Individual data objects acquisition.	NA
	SPT-CA-32 Perform back-to-back acquisitions, check device payload for modifications.	NA
Analysis:	Expected results not achieved	

5.2.71 SPT-14 (Nokia 6350)

Test Case SPT-14 Device Seizure 5.0 build 4582.15907	
Case Summary:	SPT-14 Acquire SIM memory over supported interfaces (e.g., PC/SC reader).
Assertions:	SPT-AO-01 If a cellular forensic tool provides support for connectivity of the target SIM, then the tool shall successfully recognize the target SIM via all tool-supported interfaces (e.g., PC/SC reader, proprietary reader, Smart Phone itself).
Tester Name:	rpa
Test Host:	Morrisy
Test Date:	Mon Sep 24 07:14:19 EDT 2012
Device:	Nokia6350
Source Setup:	OS: WIN XP v5.1.2600 Interface: USB
Log Highlights:	Created by Device Seizure v5.0 Acquisition started: Mon Sep 24 07:14:19 EDT 2012 Acquisition finished: Mon Sep 24 07:17:19 EDT 2012 Media connectivity was established via supported interface

Results:		
	Assertion & Expected Result	**Actual Result**
	SPT-AO-01 SIM connectivity via supported interfaces.	as expected

Analysis:	Expected results achieved

5.2.72 SPT-15 (Nokia 6350)

Test Case SPT-15 Device Seizure 5.0 build 4582.15907	
Case Summary:	SPT-15 Attempt acquisition of a nonsupported SIM.
Assertions:	SPT-AO-02 If a cellular forensic tool attempts to connect to a nonsupported SIM, then the tool shall notify the user that the SIM is not supported.
Tester Name:	rpa
Test Host:	Morrisy
Test Date:	Mon Sep 24 07:14:35 EDT 2012
Device:	Nokia6350
Source Setup:	OS: WIN XP v5.1.2600 Interface: USB
Log Highlights:	Created by Device Seizure v5.0 Acquisition started: Mon Sep 24 07:14:35 EDT 2012 Acquisition finished: Mon Sep 24 07:17:35 EDT 2012 Identification of nonsupported media was successful

Results:		
	Assertion & Expected Result	**Actual Result**
	SPT-AO-02 Identification of nonsupported SIMs.	as expected

Analysis:	Expected results achieved

5.2.73 SPT-16 (Nokia 6350)

Test Case SPT-16 Device Seizure 5.0 build 4582.15907	
Case	SPT-16 Begin SIM acquisition and interrupt connectivity by interface

Test Case SPT-16 Device Seizure 5.0 build 4582.15907	
Summary:	disengagement.
Assertions:	SPT-AO-03 If a cellular forensic tool loses connectivity with the SIM reader, then the tool shall notify the user that connectivity has been disrupted.
Tester Name:	rpa
Test Host:	Morrisy
Test Date:	Mon Sep 24 07:15:06 EDT 2012
Device:	Nokia6350
Source Setup:	OS: WIN XP v5.1.2600 Interface: USB
Log Highlights:	Created by Device Seizure v5.0 Acquisition started: Mon Sep 24 07:15:06 EDT 2012 Acquisition finished: Mon Sep 24 07:17:50 EDT 2012 Media acquisition disruption notification was successful
Results:	

Assertion & Expected Result	Actual Result
SPT-AO-03 Notification of SIM acquisition disruption.	as expected

Analysis:	Expected results achieved

5.2.74 SPT-17 (Nokia 6350)

Test Case SPT-17 Device Seizure 5.0 build 4582.15907	
Case Summary:	SPT-17 Acquire SIM memory and review reported subscriber- and equipment-related information (i.e., SPN, ICCID, IMSI, MSISDN).
Assertions:	SPT-AO-04 If a cellular forensic tool completes acquisition of the target SIM without error, then the SPN shall be presented in a useable format. SPT-AO-05 If a cellular forensic tool completes acquisition of the target SIM without error, then the ICCID shall be presented in a useable format. SPT-AO-06 If a cellular forensic tool completes acquisition of the target SIM without error, then the IMSI shall be presented in a useable format. SPT-AO-07 If a cellular forensic tool completes acquisition of the target SIM without error, then the MSISDN shall be presented in a useable format.
Tester Name:	rpa
Test Host:	Morrisy
Test Date:	Mon Sep 24 08:23:25 EDT 2012
Device:	BlackBerry_Torch
Source Setup:	OS: WIN XP v5.1.2600 Interface: USB
Log Highlights:	Created by Device Seizure v5.0 Acquisition started: Mon Sep 24 08:23:25 EDT 2012 All subscriber related data (i.e., SPN, ICCID, IMSI, MSISDN) was acquired
Results:	

Assertion & Expected Result	Actual Result
SPT-AO-04 Acquisition of SPN.	as expected
SPT-AO-05 Acquisition of ICCID.	as expected
SPT-AO-06 Acquisition of IMSI.	as expected
SPT-AO-07 Acquisition of MSISDN.	as expected

Analysis:	Expected results achieved

5.2.75 SPT-18 (Nokia 6350)

Test Case SPT-18 Device Seizure 5.0 build 4582.15907	
Case	SPT-18 Acquire SIM memory and review reported Abbreviated Dialing Numbers

Test Case SPT-18 Device Seizure 5.0 build 4582.15907	
Summary:	(ADN).
Assertions:	SPT-AO-08 If a cellular forensic tool completes acquisition of the target SIM without error, then ASCII Abbreviated Dialing Numbers (ADN) shall be presented in a useable format. SPT-AO-09 If a cellular forensic tool completes acquisition of the target SIM without error, then maximum length ADNs shall be presented in a useable format. SPT-AO-10 If a cellular forensic tool completes acquisition of the SIM without error, then ADNs containing special characters shall be presented in a useable format. SPT-AO-11 If a cellular forensic tool completes acquisition of the SIM without error, then ADNs containing blank names shall be presented in a useable format.
Tester Name:	rpa
Test Host:	Morrisy
Test Date:	Mon Sep 24 07:19:07 EDT 2012
Device:	Nokia6350
Source Setup:	OS: WIN XP v5.1.2600 Interface: USB
Log Highlights:	Created by Device Seizure v5.0 Acquisition started: Mon Sep 24 07:19:07 EDT 2012 Acquisition finished: Mon Sep 24 07:34:24 EDT 2012 All ADNs were acquired

Results:		
	Assertion & Expected Result	Actual Result
	SPT-AO-08 Acquisition of ADNs.	as expected
	SPT-AO-09 Acquisition of maximum length ADNs.	as expected
	SPT-AO-10 Acquisition of special character ADNs.	as expected
	SPT-AO-11 Acquisition of blank name ADNs.	as expected

Analysis:	Expected results achieved

5.2.76 SPT-19 (Nokia 6350)

Test Case SPT-19 Device Seizure 5.0 build 4582.15907	
Case Summary:	SPT-19 Acquire SIM memory and review reported Last Numbers Dialed (LND).
Assertions:	SPT-AO-12 If a cellular forensic tool completes acquisition of the target SIM without error, then Last Numbers Dialed (LND) shall be presented in a useable format. SPT-AO-13 If a cellular forensic tool completes acquisition of the target SIM without error, then the corresponding date/time stamps for LNDs shall be presented in a useable format.
Tester Name:	rpa
Test Host:	Morrisy
Test Date:	Mon Sep 24 07:19:32 EDT 2012
Device:	Nokia6350
Source Setup:	OS: WIN XP v5.1.2600 Interface: USB
Log Highlights:	Created by Device Seizure v5.0 Acquisition started: Mon Sep 24 07:19:32 EDT 2012 Acquisition finished: Mon Sep 24 07:34:36 EDT 2012 LNDs were acquired Date/Time Stamps correctly reported for LNDs

Results:		
	Assertion & Expected Result	Actual Result
	SPT-AO-12 Acquisition of LNDs.	as expected
	SPT-AO-13 Acquisition of LND date/time stamps.	as expected

Test Case SPT-19 Device Seizure 5.0 build 4582.15907	
Analysis:	Expected results achieved

5.2.77 SPT-20 (Nokia 6350)

Test Case SPT-20 Device Seizure 5.0 build 4582.15907	
Case Summary:	SPT-20 Acquire SIM memory and review reported text messages (SMS, EMS).
Assertions:	SPT-AO-14 If a cellular forensic tool completes acquisition of the target SIM without error, then ASCII SMS text messages shall be presented in a useable format. SPT-AO-15 If a cellular forensic tool completes acquisition of the target SIM without error, then ASCII EMS text messages shall be presented in a useable format. SPT-AO-16 If a cellular forensic tool completes acquisition of the target SIM without error, then the corresponding date/time stamps for all text messages shall be presented in a useable format. SPT-AO-17 If a cellular forensic tool completes acquisition of the target SIM without error, then the corresponding status (i.e., read, unread) for text messages shall be presented in a useable format. SPT-AO-18 If a cellular forensic tool completes acquisition of the target SIM without error, then the corresponding sender / recipient phone numbers for text messages shall be presented in a useable format.
Tester Name:	rpa
Test Host:	Morrisy
Test Date:	Mon Sep 24 07:35:10 EDT 2012
Device:	Nokia6350
Source Setup:	OS: WIN XP v5.1.2600 Interface: USB
Log Highlights:	Created by Device Seizure v5.0 Acquisition started: Mon Sep 24 07:35:10 EDT 2012 Acquisition finished: Mon Sep 24 07:38:27 EDT 2012 ALL text messages (SMS, EMS) were acquired All date/time stamps were reported for text messages Correct status flags were reported for text messages Sender and Recipient phone numbers associated with text messages were correctly reported

Results:		
	Assertion & Expected Result	**Actual Result**
	SPT-AO-14 Acquisition of SMS messages.	as expected
	SPT-AO-15 Acquisition of EMS messages.	as expected
	SPT-AO-16 Acquisition of text message date/time stamps.	as expected
	SPT-AO-17 Acquisition of text message status flags.	as expected
	SPT-AO-18 Acquisition of sender/recipient phone number associated with text messages.	as expected

Analysis:	Expected results achieved

5.2.78 SPT-21 (Nokia 6350)

Test Case SPT-21 Device Seizure 5.0 build 4582.15907	
Case Summary:	SPT-21 Acquire SIM memory and review recoverable deleted text messages (SMS, EMS).
Assertions:	SPT-AO-19 If the cellular forensic tool completes acquisition of the target SIM without error, then deleted text messages that have not been overwritten shall be presented in a useable format.
Tester Name:	rpa

Test Case SPT-21 Device Seizure 5.0 build 4582.15907	
Test Host:	Morrisy
Test Date:	Mon Sep 24 07:35:27 EDT 2012
Device:	Nokia6350
Source Setup:	OS: WIN XP v5.1.2600 Interface: USB
Log Highlights:	Created by Device Seizure v5.0 Acquisition started: Mon Sep 24 07:35:27 EDT 2012 Acquisition finished: Mon Sep 24 07:39:13 EDT 2012 Deleted text message data was recovered
Results:	

Assertion & Expected Result	Actual Result
SPT-AO-19 Acquisition of non-overwritten deleted text messages.	as expected

Analysis:	Expected results achieved

5.2.79 SPT-22 (Nokia 6350)

Test Case SPT-22 Device Seizure 5.0 build 4582.15907	
Case Summary:	SPT-22 Acquire SIM memory and review reported location-related data (i.e., LOCI, GPRSLOCI).
Assertions:	SPT-AO-20 If a cellular forensic tool completes acquisition of the target SIM without error, then location-related data (i.e., LOCI) shall be presented in a useable format. SPT-AO-21 If a cellular forensic tool completes acquisition of the target SIM without error, then location-related data (i.e., GRPSLOCI) shall be presented in a useable format.
Tester Name:	rpa
Test Host:	Morrisy
Test Date:	Mon Sep 24 07:35:46 EDT 2012
Device:	Nokia6350
Source Setup:	OS: WIN XP v5.1.2600 Interface: USB
Log Highlights:	Created by Device Seizure v5.0 Acquisition started: Mon Sep 24 07:35:46 EDT 2012 Acquisition finished: Mon Sep 24 07:39:30 EDT 2012 LOCI data was acquired GPRSLOCI data was acquired
Results:	

Assertion & Expected Result	Actual Result
SPT-AO-20 Acquisition of LOCI information.	as expected
SPT-AO-21 Acquisition of GPRSLOCI information.	as expected

Analysis:	Expected results achieved

5.2.80 SPT-23 (Nokia 6350)

Test Case SPT-23 Device Seizure 5.0 build 4582.15907	
Case Summary:	SPT-23 Acquire SIM memory by selecting a combination of supported data elements.
Assertions:	SPT-AO-01 If a cellular forensic tool provides support for connectivity of the target SIM, then the tool shall successfully recognize the target SIM via all tool-supported interfaces (e.g., PC/SC reader, proprietary reader, Smart Phone itself). SPT-AO-22 If a cellular forensic tool provides the user with an "Acquire

Test Case SPT-23 Device Seizure 5.0 build 4582.15907	
	All" SIM data objects acquisition option, then the tool shall complete the acquisition of all data objects without error. SPT-AO-23 If a cellular forensic tool provides the user with an "Select All" individual SIM data objects, then the tool shall complete the acquisition of all individually selected data objects without error. SPT-AO-24 If a cellular forensic tool provides the user with the ability to "Select Individual" SIM data objects for acquisition, then the tool shall acquire each exclusive data object without error.
Tester Name:	rpa
Test Host:	Morrisy
Test Date:	Mon Sep 24 07:40:18 EDT 2012
Device:	Nokia6350
Source Setup:	OS: WIN XP v5.1.2600 Interface: USB
Log Highlights:	Created by Device Seizure v5.0 Acquisition started: Mon Sep 24 07:40:18 EDT 2012 Acquisition finished: Mon Sep 24 07:47:02 EDT 2012 Acquire All acquisition was successful
Results:	

Assertion & Expected Result	Actual Result
SPT-AO-01 SIM connectivity via supported interfaces.	as expected
SPT-AO-22 Acquire-All data objects acquisition.	as expected
SPT-AO-23 Select-All data objects acquisition.	as expected
SPT-AO-24 Select-Individual data objects acquisition.	as expected

Analysis:	Expected results achieved

5.2.81 SPT-26 (Nokia 6350)

Test Case SPT-26 Device Seizure 5.0 build 4582.15907	
Case Summary:	SPT-26 Acquire SIM memory and review reported data via supported generated report formats.
Assertions:	SPT-AO-25 If a cellular forensic tool completes acquisition of the SIM without error, then the tool shall present the acquired data in a useable format via supported generated report formats.
Tester Name:	rpa
Test Host:	Morrisy
Test Date:	Mon Sep 24 07:40:39 EDT 2012
Device:	Nokia6350
Source Setup:	OS: WIN XP v5.1.2600 Interface: USB
Log Highlights:	Created by Device Seizure v5.0 Acquisition started: Mon Sep 24 07:40:39 EDT 2012 Acquisition finished: Mon Sep 24 07:47:17 EDT 2012 Complete representation of known data via generated reports was successful
Results:	

Assertion & Expected Result	Actual Result
SPT-AO-25 Comparison of known device data elements via generated reports.	as expected

Analysis:	Expected results achieved

5.2.82 SPT-27 (Nokia 6350)

Test Case SPT-27 Device Seizure 5.0 build 4582.15907	
Case Summary:	SPT-27 Acquire SIM memory and review reported data via the preview pane.
Assertions:	SPT-AO-26 If a cellular forensic tool completes acquisition of the SIM without error, then the tool shall present the acquired data in a useable format in a preview pane view.
Tester Name:	rpa
Test Host:	Morrisy
Test Date:	Mon Sep 24 07:41:15 EDT 2012
Device:	Nokia6350
Source Setup:	OS: WIN XP v5.1.2600 Interface: USB
Log Highlights:	Created by Device Seizure v5.0 Acquisition started: Mon Sep 24 07:41:15 EDT 2012 Acquisition finished: Mon Sep 24 07:48:02 EDT 2012 Complete representation of known data via preview pane was successful
Results:	

Assertion & Expected Result	Actual Result
SPT-AO-26 Comparison of known device data elements via preview pane.	as expected

Analysis:	Expected results achieved

5.2.83 SPT-28 (Nokia 6350)

Test Case SPT-28 Device Seizure 5.0 build 4582.15907	
Case Summary:	SPT-28 Attempt acquisition of a password-protected SIM.
Assertions:	SPT-AO-28 If the SIM is password-protected, then the cellular forensic tool shall provide the examiner with the opportunity to input the PIN before acquisition.
Tester Name:	rpa
Test Host:	Morrisy
Test Date:	Mon Sep 24 07:41:55 EDT 2012
Device:	Nokia6350
Source Setup:	OS: WIN XP v5.1.2600 Interface: USB
Log Highlights:	Created by Device Seizure v5.0 Acquisition started: Mon Sep 24 07:41:55 EDT 2012 Acquisition finished: Mon Sep 24 07:48:30 EDT 2012 Ability to enter PIN on protected media before acquisition was successful
Results:	

Assertion & Expected Result	Actual Result
SPT-AO-28 Acquisition of password-protected SIM.	as expected

Analysis:	Expected results achieved

5.2.84 SPT-30 (Nokia 6350)

Test Case SPT-30 Device Seizure 5.0 build 4582.15907	
Case Summary:	SPT-30 After a successful SIM acquisition, alter the case file via third-party means and attempt to reopen the case.
Assertions:	SPT-AO-27 If the case file or individual data objects are modified via

Test Case SPT-30 Device Seizure 5.0 build 4582.15907	
	third-party means, then the tool shall provide protection mechanisms disallowing or reporting data modification.
Tester Name:	rpa
Test Host:	Morrisy
Test Date:	Mon Sep 24 07:42:17 EDT 2012
Device:	Nokia6350
Source Setup:	OS: WIN XP v5.1.2600 Interface: USB
Log Highlights:	Created by Device Seizure v5.0 Acquisition started: Mon Sep 24 07:42:17 EDT 2012 Acquisition finished: Mon Sep 24 07:48:56 EDT 2012 Notification of modified SIM data was successful
Results:	

Assertion & Expected Result	Actual Result
SPT-AO-27 Notification of modified device case data.	as expected

Analysis:	Expected results achieved

5.2.85 SPT-34 (Nokia 6350)

Test Case SPT-34 Device Seizure 5.0 build 4582.15907	
Case Summary:	SPT-34 Acquire SIM memory and review data containing non-ASCII characters.
Assertions:	SPT-AO-40 If the cellular forensic tool supports display of non-ASCII characters, then the application should present ADNs in their native format. SPT-AO-41 If the cellular forensic tool supports proper display of non-ASCII characters, then the application should present text messages in their native format.
Tester Name:	rpa
Test Host:	Morrisy
Test Date:	Mon Sep 24 07:42:37 EDT 2012
Device:	Nokia6350
Source Setup:	OS: WIN XP v5.1.2600 Interface: USB
Log Highlights:	Created by Device Seizure v5.0 Acquisition started: Mon Sep 24 07:42:37 EDT 2012 Acquisition finished: Mon Sep 24 07:49:11 EDT 2012 Non-ASCII ADNs were acquired and properly displayed Non-ASCII text messages were acquired and properly displayed
Results:	

Assertion & Expected Result	Actual Result
SPT-AO-40 Acquisition of non-ASCII address book entries/ADNs.	as expected
SPT-AO-41 Acquisition of non-ASCII text messages.	as expected

Analysis:	Expected results achieved

5.2.86 SPT-35 (Nokia 6350)

Test Case SPT-35 Device Seizure 5.0 build 4582.15907	
Case Summary:	SPT-35 Begin acquisition on a PIN protected SIM to determine if the tool provides an accurate count of the remaining number of PIN attempts and if the PIN attempts are decremented when entering an incorrect value.

Test Case SPT-35 Device Seizure 5.0 build 4582.15907	
Assertions:	SPT-AO-29 If a cellular forensic tool provides the examiner with the remaining number of authentication attempts, then the application should provide an accurate count of the remaining PIN attempts.
Tester Name:	rpa
Test Host:	Morrisy
Test Date:	Mon Sep 24 07:43:00 EDT 2012
Device:	Nokia6350
Source Setup:	OS: WIN XP v5.1.2600 Interface: USB
Log Highlights:	Created by Device Seizure v5.0 Acquisition started: Mon Sep 24 07:43:00 EDT 2012 Acquisition finished: Mon Sep 24 07:49:40 EDT 2012 The remaining number of PIN attempts were properly displayed
Results:	

Assertion & Expected Result	Actual Result
SPT-AO-29 Display remaining number of PIN attempts.	as expected

Analysis:	Expected results achieved

5.2.87 SPT-36 (Nokia 6350)

Test Case SPT-36 Device Seizure 5.0 build 4582.15907	
Case Summary:	SPT-36 Begin acquisition on a SIM whose PIN attempts have been exhausted to determine if the tool provides an accurate count of the remaining number of PUK attempts and if the PUK attempts are decremented when entering an incorrect value.
Assertions:	SPT-AO-30 If a cellular forensic tool provides the examiner with the remaining number of PUK attempts, then the application should provide an accurate count of the remaining PUK attempts.
Tester Name:	rpa
Test Host:	Morrisy
Test Date:	Mon Sep 24 07:43:28 EDT 2012
Device:	Nokia6350
Source Setup:	OS: WIN XP v5.1.2600 Interface: USB
Log Highlights:	Created by Device Seizure v5.0 Acquisition started: Mon Sep 24 07:43:28 EDT 2012 Acquisition finished: Mon Sep 24 07:49:57 EDT 2012 Remaining number of PUK attempts were properly displayed
Results:	

Assertion & Expected Result	Actual Result
SPT-AO-30 Display remaining number of PUK attempts.	as expected

Analysis:	Expected results achieved

5.2.88 SPT-39 (Nokia 6350)

Test Case SPT-39 Device Seizure 5.0 build 4582.15907	
Case Summary:	SPT-39 Acquire SIM memory and review hash values for vendor supported data objects.
Assertions:	SPT-AO-43 If the cellular forensic tool supports hashing for individual data objects, then the tool shall present the user with a hash value for each supported data object.
Tester Name:	rpa

Test Case SPT-39 Device Seizure 5.0 build 4582.15907	
Test Host:	Morrisy
Test Date:	Mon Sep 24 07:43:48 EDT 2012
Device:	Nokia6350
Source Setup:	OS: WIN XP v5.1.2600 Interface: USB
Log Highlights:	Created by Device Seizure v5.0 Acquisition started: Mon Sep 24 07:43:48 EDT 2012 Acquisition finished: Mon Sep 24 07:50:12 EDT 2012 Hash values were properly reported for individually acquired SIM data elements
Results:	

Assertion & Expected Result	Actual Result
SPT-AO-43 Acquire data, check known hash values for consistency.	as expected

Analysis:	Expected results achieved

5.2.89 SPT-01 (iPhone4 CDMA)

Test Case SPT-01 Device Seizure 5.0 build 4582.15907	
Case Summary:	SPT-01 Acquire mobile device internal memory over tool-supported interfaces (e.g., cable, Bluetooth, IrDA).
Assertions:	SPT-CA-01 If a cellular forensic tool provides support for connectivity of the target device, then the tool shall successfully recognize the target device via all vendor supported interfaces (e.g., cable, Bluetooth, IrDA). SPT-CA-04 If a cellular forensic tool completes acquisition of the target device without error, then the tool shall have the ability to present acquired data objects in a useable format via either a preview pane or generated report. SPT-CA-29 If a cellular forensic tool provides the user with an "Acquire All" device data objects acquisition option, then the tool shall complete the acquisition of all data objects without error. SPT-CA-30 If a cellular forensic tool provides the user with a "Select All" individual device data objects, then the tool shall complete the acquisition of all individually selected data objects without error. SPT-CA-31 If a cellular forensic tool provides the user with the ability to "Select Individual" device data objects for acquisition, then the tool shall acquire each exclusive data object without error. SPT-CA-32 If a cellular forensic tool completes two consecutive logical acquisitions of the target device without error, then the payload (data objects) on the mobile device shall remain consistent.
Tester Name:	rpa
Test Host:	Morrisy
Test Date:	Tue Sep 25 07:09:57 EDT 2012
Device:	iPhone4 CDMA
Source Setup:	OS: WIN XP v5.1.2600 Interface: cable
Log Highlights:	Created by Device Seizure v5.0 Acquisition started: Tue Sep 25 07:09:57 EDT 2012 Acquisition finished: Tue Sep 25 07:13:14 EDT 2012 Device connectivity was established via supported interface
Results:	

Assertion & Expected Result	Actual Result
SPT-CA-01 Device connectivity via supported interfaces.	as expected
SPT-CA-04 Readability and completeness of acquired data via supported reports.	as expected

Test Case SPT-01 Device Seizure 5.0 build 4582.15907		
	SPT-CA-29 Acquire-All data objects acquisition.	as expected
	SPT-CA-30 Select-All data objects acquisition.	as expected
	SPT-CA-31 Select-Individual data objects acquisition.	as expected
	SPT-CA-32 Perform back-to-back acquisitions, check device payload for modifications.	as expected
Analysis:	Expected results achieved	

5.2.90 SPT-02 (iPhone4 CDMA)

Test Case SPT-02 Device Seizure 5.0 build 4582.15907	
Case Summary:	SPT-02 Attempt internal memory acquisition of a nonsupported mobile device.
Assertions:	SPT-CA-02 If a cellular forensic tool attempts to connect to a nonsupported device, then the tool shall notify the user that the device is not supported.
Tester Name:	rpa
Test Host:	Morrisy
Test Date:	Tue Sep 25 07:10:20 EDT 2012
Device:	unsupported device
Source Setup:	OS: WIN XP v5.1.2600 Interface: cable
Log Highlights:	Created by Device Seizure v5.0 Acquisition started: Tue Sep 25 07:10:20 EDT 2012 Acquisition finished: Tue Sep 25 07:13:30 EDT 2012 Identification of nonsupported devices was successful
Results:	

Assertion & Expected Result	Actual Result
SPT-CA-02 Identification of nonsupported devices.	as expected

Analysis:	Expected results achieved

5.2.91 SPT-03 (iPhone4 CDMA)

Test Case SPT-03 Device Seizure 5.0 build 4582.15907	
Case Summary:	SPT-03 Begin mobile device internal memory acquisition and interrupt connectivity by interface disengagement.
Assertions:	SPT-CA-03 If connectivity between the mobile device and cellular forensic tool is disrupted, then the tool shall notify the user that connectivity has been disrupted.
Tester Name:	rpa
Test Host:	Morrisy
Test Date:	Tue Sep 25 07:15:07 EDT 2012
Device:	iPhone4 CDMA
Source Setup:	OS: WIN XP v5.1.2600 Interface: cable
Log Highlights:	Created by Device Seizure v5.0 Acquisition started: Tue Sep 25 07:15:07 EDT 2012 Acquisition finished: Tue Sep 25 07:18:22 EDT 2012 Device acquisition disruption notification was successful
Results:	

Assertion & Expected Result	Actual Result
SPT-CA-03 Notification of device acquisition disruption.	as expected

Test Case SPT-03 Device Seizure 5.0 build 4582.15907	
Analysis:	Expected results achieved

5.2.92 SPT-04 (iPhone4 CDMA)

Test Case SPT-04 Device Seizure 5.0 build 4582.15907	
Case Summary:	SPT-04 Acquire mobile device internal memory and review reported data via the preview pane or generated reports for readability.
Assertions:	SPT-CA-04 If a cellular forensic tool completes acquisition of the target device without error, then the tool shall have the ability to present acquired data objects in a useable format via either a preview pane or generated report.
Tester Name:	rpa
Test Host:	Morrisy
Test Date:	Tue Sep 25 07:18:52 EDT 2012
Device:	iPhone4_CDMA
Source Setup:	OS: WIN XP v5.1.2600 Interface: cable
Log Highlights:	Created by Device Seizure v5.0 Acquisition started: Tue Sep 25 07:18:52 EDT 2012 Acquisition finished: Tue Sep 25 07:23:03 EDT 2012 Readability and completeness of acquired data was successful

Results:	Assertion & Expected Result	Actual Result
	SPT-CA-04 Readability and completeness of acquired data via supported reports.	as expected

Analysis:	Expected results achieved

5.2.93 SPT-05 (iPhone4 CDMA)

Test Case SPT-05 Device Seizure 5.0 build 4582.15907	
Case Summary:	SPT-05 Acquire mobile device internal memory and review reported subscriber- and equipment-related information (e.g., IMEI/MEID/ESN, MSISDN).
Assertions:	SPT-CA-05 If a cellular forensic tool completes acquisition of the target device without error, then subscriber related information shall be presented in a useable format. SPT-CA-06 If a cellular forensic tool completes acquisition of the target device without error, then equipment-related information shall be presented in a useable format.
Tester Name:	rpa
Test Host:	Morrisy
Test Date:	Tue Sep 25 07:19:17 EDT 2012
Device:	iPhone4 CDMA
Source Setup:	OS: WIN XP v5.1.2600 Interface: cable
Log Highlights:	Created by Device Seizure v5.0 Acquisition started: Tue Sep 25 07:19:17 EDT 2012 Acquisition finished: Tue Sep 25 07:23:19 EDT 2012 MSISDN was not reported IMEI, MEID/ESN were not acquired

Results:	Assertion & Expected Result	Actual Result
	SPT-CA-05 Acquisition of MSISDN, IMSI.	Not as expected

Test Case SPT-05 Device Seizure 5.0 build 4582.15907	
	SPT-CA-06 Acquisition of IMEI/MEID/ESN. Not as expected
Analysis:	Expected results not achieved

5.2.94 SPT-06 (iPhone4 CDMA)

Test Case SPT-06 Device Seizure 5.0 build 4582.15907	
Case Summary:	SPT-06 Acquire mobile device internal memory and review reported PIM-related data.
Assertions:	SPT-CA-07 If a cellular forensic tool completes acquisition of the target device without error, then address book entries shall be presented in a useable format. SPT-CA-08 If a cellular forensic tool completes acquisition of the target device without error, then maximum length address book entries shall be presented in a useable format. SPT-CA-09 If a cellular forensic tool completes acquisition of the target device without error, then address book entries containing special characters shall be presented in a useable format. SPT-CA-10 If a cellular forensic tool completes acquisition of the target device without error, then address book entries containing blank names shall be presented in a useable format. SPT-CA-11 If a cellular forensic tool completes acquisition of the target device without error, then email addresses associated with address book entries shall be presented in a useable format. SPT-CA-12 If a cellular forensic tool completes acquisition of the target device without error, then graphics associated with address book entries shall be presented in a useable format. SPT-CA-13 If a cellular forensic tool completes acquisition of the target device without error, then datebook, calendar, note entries shall be presented in a useable format. SPT-CA-14 If a cellular forensic tool completes acquisition of the target device without error, then maximum length datebook, calendar, note entries shall be presented in a useable format.
Tester Name:	rpa
Test Host:	Morrisy
Test Date:	Tue Sep 25 07:23:58 EDT 2012
Device:	iPhone4 CDMA
Source Setup:	OS: WIN XP v5.1.2600 Interface: cable
Log Highlights:	Created by Device Seizure v5.0 Acquisition started: Tue Sep 25 07:23:58 EDT 2012 Acquisition finished: Tue Sep 25 07:39:38 EDT 2012 Regular Length Address Book entries were acquired Maximum Length Address Book entries were acquired Special Character Address Book entries were acquired Blank Name Address Book entries were acquired Email addresses within Address Book entries were acquired Embedded graphics within Address Book entries were not acquired ALL PIM-related data was acquired **Notes:** Graphics files associated with address book entries were not reported.

Results:	Assertion & Expected Result	Actual Result
	SPT-CA-07 Acquisition of address book entries.	as expected
	SPT-CA-08 Acquisition of maximum length address book entries.	as expected
	SPT-CA-09 Acquisition of address book entries containing special characters.	as expected
	SPT-CA-10 Acquisition of address book entries containing a blank name entry.	as expected

Test Case SPT-06 Device Seizure 5.0 build 4582.15907		
	SPT-CA-11 Acquisition of embedded email addresses within address book entries.	as expected
	SPT-CA-12 Acquisition of embedded graphics within address book entries.	Not as expected
	SPT-CA-13 Acquisition of PIM data (i.e., datebook/calendar, notes).	as expected
	SPT-CA-14 Acquisition of maximum length PIM data.	as expected
Analysis:	Partial results achieved	

5.2.95 SPT-07 (iPhone4 CDMA)

Test Case SPT-07 Device Seizure 5.0 build 4582.15907	
Case Summary:	SPT-07 Acquire mobile device internal memory and review reported call logs.
Assertions:	SPT-CA-15 If a cellular forensic tool completes acquisition of the target device without error, then call logs (incoming/outgoing/missed) shall be presented in a useable format. SPT-CA-16 If a cellular forensic tool completes acquisition of the target device without error, then the corresponding date/time stamps and the duration of the call for call logs shall be presented in a useable format.
Tester Name:	rpa
Test Host:	Morrisy
Test Date:	Tue Sep 25 07:24:19 EDT 2012
Device:	iPhone4 CDMA
Source Setup:	OS: WIN XP v5.1.2600 Interface: cable
Log Highlights:	Created by Device Seizure v5.0 Acquisition started: Tue Sep 25 07:24:19 EDT 2012 Acquisition finished: Tue Sep 25 07:40:52 EDT 2012 All Call Logs (incoming, outgoing, missed) were acquired All Call Log date/time stamps data were correctly reported **Notes**: Missed calls were categorized as Incoming calls.
Results:	

Assertion & Expected Result	Actual Result
SPT-CA-15 Acquisition of call logs.	Not as expected
SPT-CA-16 Acquisition of call log date/time stamps.	as expected

Analysis:	Partial results achieved

5.2.96 SPT-08 (iPhone4 CDMA)

Test Case SPT-08 Device Seizure 5.0 build 4582.15907	
Case Summary:	SPT-08 Acquire mobile device internal memory and review reported text messages.
Assertions:	SPT-CA-17 If a cellular forensic tool completes acquisition of the target device without error, then ASCII text messages (i.e., SMS, EMS) shall be presented in a useable format. SPT-CA-18 If a cellular forensic tool completes acquisition of the target device without error, then the corresponding date/time stamps for text messages shall be presented in a useable format. SPT-CA-19 If a cellular forensic tool completes acquisition of the target device without error, then the corresponding status (i.e., read, unread) for text messages shall be presented in a useable format. SPT-CA-20 If a cellular forensic tool completes acquisition of the target device without error, then the corresponding sender / recipient phone numbers for text messages shall be presented in a useable format.

Test Case SPT-08 Device Seizure 5.0 build 4582.15907	
Tester Name:	rpa
Test Host:	Morrisy
Test Date:	Tue Sep 25 07:24:40 EDT 2012
Device:	iPhone4 CDMA
Source Setup:	OS: WIN XP v5.1.2600 Interface: cable
Log Highlights:	Created by Device Seizure v5.0 Acquisition started: Tue Sep 25 07:24:40 EDT 2012 Acquisition finished: Tue Sep 25 07:43:38 EDT 2012 ALL text messages (SMS, EMS) were acquired Correct date/time stamps were reported for all text messages Partial status flags were reported for text messages Sender and Recipient phone numbers associated with text messages were correctly reported **Notes**: Unread text messages were not assigned a Type i.e., UNREAD

Results:	Assertion & Expected Result	Actual Result
	SPT-CA-17 Acquisition of text messages.	as expected
	SPT-CA-18 Acquisition of text message date/time stamps.	as expected
	SPT-CA-19 Acquisition of text message status flags.	Not as expected
	SPT-CA-20 Acquisition of sender/recipient phone number associated with text messages.	as expected
Analysis:	Partial results achieved	

5.2.97 SPT-09 (iPhone4 CDMA)

Test Case SPT-09 Device Seizure 5.0 build 4582.15907	
Case Summary:	SPT-09 Acquire mobile device internal memory and review reported MMS multi-media-related data (i.e., text, audio, graphics, video).
Assertions:	SPT-CA-21 If a cellular forensic tool completes acquisition of the target device without error, then MMS messages and associated audio shall be presented in a useable format. SPT-CA-22 If a cellular forensic tool completes acquisition of the target device without error, then MMS messages and associated graphic files shall be presented in a useable format. SPT-CA-23 If a cellular forensic tool completes acquisition of the target device without error, then MMS messages and associated video shall be presented in a useable format.
Tester Name:	rpa
Test Host:	Morrisy
Test Date:	Tue Sep 25 07:58:34 EDT 2012
Device:	iPhone4 CDMA
Source Setup:	OS: WIN XP v5.1.2600 Interface: cable
Log Highlights:	Created by Device Seizure v5.0 Acquisition started: Tue Sep 25 07:58:34 EDT 2012 Acquisition finished: Tue Sep 25 07:59:55 EDT 2012 Partial audio MMS messages were acquired Image MMS messages were acquired Video MMS messages were acquired **Notes**: Sound bytes attached to MMS messages were not reported.

	The textual portion of the MMS messages is blank and has to be searched for in the sms.db file.	
Results:	**Assertion & Expected Result**	**Actual Result**
	SPT-CA-21 Acquisition of audio MMS messages.	Not as expected
	SPT-CA-22 Acquisition of graphic data image MMS messages.	Not as expected
	SPT-CA-23 Acquisition of video MMS messages.	Not as expected
Analysis:	Expected results not achieved	

5.2.98 SPT-10 (iPhone4 CDMA)

Test Case SPT-10 Device Seizure 5.0 build 4582.15907

Case Summary:	SPT-10 Acquire mobile device internal memory and review reported stand-alone multi-media data (i.e., audio, graphics, video).
Assertions:	SPT-CA-24 If a cellular forensic tool completes acquisition of the target device without error, then stand-alone audio files shall be presented in a useable format via either an internal application or suggested third-party application. SPT-CA-25 If a cellular forensic tool completes acquisition of the target device without error, then stand-alone graphic files shall be presented in a useable format via either an internal application or suggested third-party application. SPT-CA-26 If a cellular forensic tool completes acquisition of the target device without error, then stand-alone video files shall be presented in a useable format via either an internal application or suggested third-party application.
Tester Name:	rpa
Test Host:	Morrisy
Test Date:	Tue Sep 25 07:55:58 EDT 2012
Device:	iPhone4 CDMA
Source Setup:	OS: WIN XP v5.1.2600 Interface: cable
Log Highlights:	Created by Device Seizure v5.0 Acquisition started: Tue Sep 25 07:55:58 EDT 2012 Acquisition finished: Tue Sep 25 07:56:36 EDT 2012 Audio files were not acquired Image files were acquired Video files were not acquired
Results:	**Assertion & Expected Result**	**Actual Result**
	SPT-CA-24 Acquisition of stand-alone audio files.	Not as expected
	SPT-CA-25 Acquisition of stand-alone graphic files.	as expected
	SPT-CA-26 Acquisition of stand-alone video files.	Not as expected
Analysis:	Partial results achieved	

5.2.99 SPT-12 (iPhone4 CDMA)

Test Case SPT-12 Device Seizure 5.0 build 4582.15907

Test Case SPT-12 Device Seizure 5.0 build 4582.15907	
Case Summary:	SPT-12 Acquire mobile device internal memory and review Internet-related data (i.e., bookmarks, visited sites.
Assertions:	SPT-CA-28 If a cellular forensic tool completes acquisition of the target device without error, then Internet-related data (i.e., bookmarks, visited sites) cached to the device shall be acquired and presented in a useable format.
Tester Name:	rpa
Test Host:	Morrisy
Test Date:	Tue Sep 25 07:46:42 EDT 2012
Device:	iPhone4 CDMA
Source Setup:	OS: WIN XP v5.1.2600 Interface: cable
Log Highlights:	Created by Device Seizure v5.0 Acquisition started: Tue Sep 25 07:46:42 EDT 2012 Acquisition finished: Tue Sep 25 07:48:49 EDT 2012 All Internet-related data was acquired
Results:	

Assertion & Expected Result	Actual Result
SPT-CA-28 Acquisition of Internet-related data.	as expected

Analysis:	Expected results achieved

5.2.100 SPT-13 (iPhone4 CDMA)

Test Case SPT-13 Device Seizure 5.0 build 4582.15907	
Case Summary:	SPT-13 Acquire mobile device internal memory by selecting a combination of supported data elements.
Assertions:	SPT-CA-29 If a cellular forensic tool provides the user with an "Acquire All" device data objects acquisition option, then the tool shall complete the acquisition of all data objects without error. SPT-CA-30 If a cellular forensic tool provides the user with an "Select All" individual device data objects, then the tool shall complete the acquisition of all individually selected data objects without error. SPT-CA-31 If a cellular forensic tool provides the user with the ability to "Select Individual" device data objects for acquisition, then the tool shall acquire each exclusive data object without error.
Tester Name:	rpa
Test Host:	Morrisy
Test Date:	Tue Sep 25 07:47:01 EDT 2012
Device:	iPhone4 CDMA
Source Setup:	OS: WIN XP v5.1.2600 Interface: cable
Log Highlights:	Created by Device Seizure v5.0 Acquisition started: Tue Sep 25 07:47:01 EDT 2012 Acquisition finished: Tue Sep 25 07:49:03 EDT 2012 Acquire All acquisition was successful
Results:	

Assertion & Expected Result	Actual Result
SPT-CA-29 Acquire-All data objects acquisition.	as expected
SPT-CA-30 Select-All data objects acquisition.	as expected
SPT-CA-31 Select-Individual data objects acquisition.	as expected

Analysis:	Expected results achieved

5.2.101 SPT-24 (iPhone4 CDMA)

Test Case SPT-24 Device Seizure 5.0 build 4582.15907	
Case Summary:	SPT-24 Acquire mobile device internal memory and review reported data via supported generated report formats.
Assertions:	SPT-AO-25 If a cellular forensic tool completes acquisition of the target device without error, then the tool shall present the acquired data in a useable format via supported generated report formats.
Tester Name:	rpa
Test Host:	Morrisy
Test Date:	Tue Sep 25 07:49:37 EDT 2012
Device:	iPhone4_CDMA
Source Setup:	OS: WIN XP v5.1.2600 Interface: cable
Log Highlights:	Created by Device Seizure v5.0 Acquisition started: Tue Sep 25 07:49:37 EDT 2012 Acquisition finished: Tue Sep 25 07:53:36 EDT 2012 Complete representation of known data via generated reports was successful
Results:	

Assertion & Expected Result	Actual Result
SPT-AO-25 Comparison of known device data elements via generated reports.	as expected

Analysis:	Expected results achieved

5.2.102 SPT-25 (iPhone4 CDMA)

Test Case SPT-25 Device Seizure 5.0 build 4582.15907	
Case Summary:	SPT-25 Acquire mobile device internal memory and review reported data via the preview pane.
Assertions:	SPT-AO-26 If a cellular forensic tool completes acquisition of the target device without error, then the tool shall present the acquired data in a useable format in a preview pane view.
Tester Name:	rpa
Test Host:	Morrisy
Test Date:	Tue Sep 25 07:49:59 EDT 2012
Device:	iPhone4_CDMA
Source Setup:	OS: WIN XP v5.1.2600 Interface: cable
Log Highlights:	Created by Device Seizure v5.0 Acquisition started: Tue Sep 25 07:49:59 EDT 2012 Acquisition finished: Tue Sep 25 07:53:58 EDT 2012 Complete representation of known data via preview pane was successful
Results:	

Assertion & Expected Result	Actual Result
SPT-AO-26 Comparison of known device data elements via preview pane.	as expected

Analysis:	Expected results achieved

5.2.103 SPT-29 (iPhone4 CDMA)

Test Case SPT-29 Device Seizure 5.0 build 4582.15907	
Case	SPT-29 After a successful mobile device internal memory, alter the case

Test Case SPT-29 Device Seizure 5.0 build 4582.15907	
Summary:	file via third-party means and attempt to reopen the case.
Assertions:	SPT-AO-27 If the case file or individual data objects are modified via third-party means, then the tool shall provide protection mechanisms disallowing or reporting data modification.
Tester Name:	rpa
Test Host:	Morrisy
Test Date:	Tue Sep 25 07:50:31 EDT 2012
Device:	iPhone4 CDMA
Source Setup:	OS: WIN XP v5.1.2600 Interface: cable
Log Highlights:	Created by Device Seizure v5.0 Acquisition started: Tue Sep 25 07:50:31 EDT 2012 Acquisition finished: Tue Sep 25 07:54:17 EDT 2012 Notification of modified device memory data was successful
Results:	

Assertion & Expected Result	Actual Result
SPT-AO-27 Notification of modified device case data.	as expected

Analysis:	Expected results achieved

5.2.104 SPT-33 (iPhone4 CDMA)

Test Case SPT-33 Device Seizure 5.0 build 4582.15907	
Case Summary:	SPT-33 Acquire mobile device internal memory and review data containing non-ASCII characters.
Assertions:	SPT-AO-40 If the cellular forensic tool supports display of non-ASCII characters, then the application should present address book entries in their native format. SPT-AO-41 If the cellular forensic tool supports proper display of non-ASCII characters, then the application should present text messages in their native format.
Tester Name:	rpa
Test Host:	Morrisy
Test Date:	Tue Sep 25 07:50:52 EDT 2012
Device:	iPhone4 CDMA
Source Setup:	OS: WIN XP v5.1.2600 Interface: cable
Log Highlights:	Created by Device Seizure v5.0 Acquisition started: Tue Sep 25 07:50:52 EDT 2012 Acquisition finished: Tue Sep 25 07:54:45 EDT 2012 Non-ASCII Address book entries were acquired and properly displayed Non-ASCII text messages were acquired and properly displayed
Results:	

Assertion & Expected Result	Actual Result
SPT-AO-40 Acquisition of non-ASCII address book entries/ADNs.	as expected
SPT-AO-41 Acquisition of non-ASCII text messages.	as expected

Analysis:	Expected results achieved

5.2.105 SPT-38 (iPhone4 CDMA)

Test Case SPT-38 Device Seizure 5.0 build 4582.15907	
Case Summary:	SPT-38 Acquire mobile device internal memory and review hash values for vendor supported data objects.

Test Case SPT-38 Device Seizure 5.0 build 4582.15907	
Assertions:	SPT-AO-43 If the cellular forensic tool supports hashing for individual data objects, then the tool shall present the user with a hash value for each supported data object.
Tester Name:	rpa
Test Host:	Morrisy
Test Date:	Tue Sep 25 07:51:11 EDT 2012
Device:	iPhone4_CDMA
Source Setup:	OS: WIN XP v5.1.2600 Interface: cable
Log Highlights:	Created by Device Seizure v5.0 Acquisition started: Tue Sep 25 07:51:11 EDT 2012 Acquisition finished: Tue Sep 25 07:55:07 EDT 2012 Hash values were properly reported for individually acquired device data elements

Results:	Assertion & Expected Result	Actual Result
	SPT-AO-43 Acquire data, check known hash values for consistency.	as expected

Analysis:	Expected results achieved

5.2.106 SPT-01 (HTC Thunderbolt)

Test Case SPT-01 Device Seizure 5.0 build 4582.15907	
Case Summary:	SPT-01 Acquire mobile device internal memory over tool-supported interfaces (e.g., cable, Bluetooth, IrDA).
Assertions:	SPT-CA-01 If a cellular forensic tool provides support for connectivity of the target device, then the tool shall successfully recognize the target device via all vendor supported interfaces (e.g., cable, Bluetooth, IrDA). SPT-CA-04 If a cellular forensic tool completes acquisition of the target device without error, then the tool shall have the ability to present acquired data objects in a useable format via either a preview pane or generated report. SPT-CA-29 If a cellular forensic tool provides the user with an "Acquire All" device data objects acquisition option, then the tool shall complete the acquisition of all data objects without error. SPT-CA-30 If a cellular forensic tool provides the user with a "Select All" individual device data objects, then the tool shall complete the acquisition of all individually selected data objects without error. SPT-CA-31 If a cellular forensic tool provides the user with the ability to "Select Individual" device data objects for acquisition, then the tool shall acquire each exclusive data object without error. SPT-CA-32 If a cellular forensic tool completes two consecutive logical acquisitions of the target device without error, then the payload (data objects) on the mobile device shall remain consistent.
Tester Name:	rpa
Test Host:	Morrisy
Test Date:	Tue Sep 25 10:02:09 EDT 2012
Device:	HTC_Thunderbolt
Source Setup:	OS: WIN XP v5.1.2600 Interface: cable
Log Highlights:	Created by Device Seizure v5.0 Acquisition started: Tue Sep 25 10:02:09 EDT 2012 Acquisition finished: Tue Sep 25 10:02:16 EDT 2012 Device connectivity was established via supported interface **Notes:** The acquisition ended in errors. The following error message was reported: Acquisition process has failed.

Test Case SPT-01 Device Seizure 5.0 build 4582.15907		
	Result: Connection broken	
Results:		
	Assertion & Expected Result	**Actual Result**
	SPT-CA-01 Device connectivity via supported interfaces.	Not as expected
	SPT-CA-04 Readability and completeness of acquired data via supported reports.	as expected
	SPT-CA-29 Acquire-All data objects acquisition.	as expected
	SPT-CA-30 Select-All data objects acquisition.	as expected
	SPT-CA-31 Select-Individual data objects acquisition.	as expected
	SPT-CA-32 Perform back-to-back acquisitions, check device payload for modifications.	as expected
Analysis:	Partial results achieved	

5.2.107 SPT-02 (HTC Thunderbolt)

Test Case SPT-02 Device Seizure 5.0 build 4582.15907	
Case Summary:	SPT-02 Attempt internal memory acquisition of a nonsupported mobile device.
Assertions:	SPT-CA-02 If a cellular forensic tool attempts to connect to a nonsupported device, then the tool shall notify the user that the device is not supported.
Tester Name:	rpa
Test Host:	Morrisy
Test Date:	Tue Sep 25 10:04:05 EDT 2012
Device:	unsupported_device
Source Setup:	OS: WIN XP v5.1.2600 Interface: cable
Log Highlights:	Created by Device Seizure v5.0 Acquisition started: Tue Sep 25 10:04:05 EDT 2012 Acquisition finished: Tue Sep 25 10:05:40 EDT 2012 Identification of nonsupported devices was successful
Results:	

Assertion & Expected Result	Actual Result
SPT-CA-02 Identification of nonsupported devices.	as expected

Analysis:	Expected results achieved

5.2.108 SPT-03 (HTC Thunderbolt)

Test Case SPT-03 Device Seizure 5.0 build 4582.15907	
Case Summary:	SPT-03 Begin mobile device internal memory acquisition and interrupt connectivity by interface disengagement.
Assertions:	SPT-CA-03 If connectivity between the mobile device and cellular forensic tool is disrupted, then the tool shall notify the user that connectivity has been disrupted.
Tester Name:	rpa
Test Host:	Morrisy
Test Date:	Tue Sep 25 10:06:37 EDT 2012
Device:	HTC Thunderbolt
Source Setup:	OS: WIN XP v5.1.2600 Interface: cable
Log Highlights:	Created by Device Seizure v5.0 Acquisition started: Tue Sep 25 10:06:37 EDT 2012

Test Case SPT-03 Device Seizure 5.0 build 4582.15907	
	Acquisition finished: Tue Sep 25 10:11:22 EDT 2012 Device acquisition disruption notification was successful
Results:	

Assertion & Expected Result	Actual Result
SPT-CA-03 Notification of device acquisition disruption.	as expected

Analysis:	Expected results achieved

5.2.109 SPT-04 (HTC Thunderbolt)

Test Case SPT-04 Device Seizure 5.0 build 4582.15907	
Case Summary:	SPT-04 Acquire mobile device internal memory and review reported data via the preview pane or generated reports for readability.
Assertions:	SPT-CA-04 If a cellular forensic tool completes acquisition of the target device without error, then the tool shall have the ability to present acquired data objects in a useable format via either a preview pane or generated report.
Tester Name:	rpa
Test Host:	Morrisy
Test Date:	Tue Sep 25 10:18:42 EDT 2012
Device:	HTC Thunderbolt
Source Setup:	OS: WIN XP v5.1.2600 Interface: cable
Log Highlights:	Created by Device Seizure v5.0 Acquisition started: Tue Sep 25 10:18:42 EDT 2012 Acquisition finished: Tue Sep 25 10:22:01 EDT 2012 Readability and completeness of acquired data was successful
Results:	

Assertion & Expected Result	Actual Result
SPT-CA-04 Readability and completeness of acquired data via supported reports.	as expected

Analysis:	Expected results achieved

5.2.110 SPT-05 (HTC Thunderbolt)

Test Case SPT-05 Device Seizure 5.0 build 4582.15907	
Case Summary:	SPT-05 Acquire mobile device internal memory and review reported subscriber and equipment-related information (e.g., IMEI/MEID/ESN, MSISDN).
Assertions:	SPT-CA-05 If a cellular forensic tool completes acquisition of the target device without error, then subscriber related information shall be presented in a useable format. SPT-CA-06 If a cellular forensic tool completes acquisition of the target device without error, then equipment-related information shall be presented in a useable format.
Tester Name:	rpa
Test Host:	Morrisy
Test Date:	Tue Sep 25 10:33:09 EDT 2012
Device:	HTC_Thunderbolt
Source Setup:	OS: WIN XP v5.1.2600 Interface: cable
Log Highlights:	Created by Device Seizure v5.0 Acquisition started: Tue Sep 25 10:33:09 EDT 2012

Test Case SPT-05 Device Seizure 5.0 build 4582.15907	
	Acquisition finished: Tue Sep 25 11:26:27 EDT 2012 IMEI, MEID/ESN were acquired
Results:	

Assertion & Expected Result	Actual Result
SPT-CA-05 Acquisition of MSISDN, IMSI.	as expected
SPT-CA-06 Acquisition of IMEI/MEID/ESN.	as expected

Analysis:	Expected results achieved

5.2.111 SPT-06 (HTC Thunderbolt)

Test Case SPT-06 Device Seizure 5.0 build 4582.15907	
Case Summary:	SPT-06 Acquire mobile device internal memory and review reported PIM-related data.
Assertions:	SPT-CA-07 If a cellular forensic tool completes acquisition of the target device without error, then address book entries shall be presented in a useable format. SPT-CA-08 If a cellular forensic tool completes acquisition of the target device without error, then maximum length address book entries shall be presented in a useable format. SPT-CA-09 If a cellular forensic tool completes acquisition of the target device without error, then address book entries containing special characters shall be presented in a useable format. SPT-CA-10 If a cellular forensic tool completes acquisition of the target device without error, then address book entries containing blank names shall be presented in a useable format. SPT-CA-11 If a cellular forensic tool completes acquisition of the target device without error, then email addresses associated with address book entries shall be presented in a useable format. SPT-CA-12 If a cellular forensic tool completes acquisition of the target device without error, then graphics associated with address book entries shall be presented in a useable format. SPT-CA-13 If a cellular forensic tool completes acquisition of the target device without error, then datebook, calendar, note entries shall be presented in a useable format. SPT-CA-14 If a cellular forensic tool completes acquisition of the target device without error, then maximum length datebook, calendar, note entries shall be presented in a useable format.
Tester Name:	rpa
Test Host:	Morrisy
Test Date:	Tue Sep 25 11:38:39 EDT 2012
Device:	HTC Thunderbolt
Source Setup:	OS: WIN XP v5.1.2600 Interface: cable
Log Highlights:	Created by Device Seizure v5.0 Acquisition started: Tue Sep 25 11:38:39 EDT 2012 Acquisition finished: Tue Sep 25 12:04:12 EDT 2012 All address book entries were successfully acquired Basic PIM-related data was not acquired Maximum length PIM-related data was not acquired **Notes:** Calendar and Memo entries were not reported.
Results:	

Assertion & Expected Result	Actual Result
SPT-CA-07 Acquisition of address book entries.	as expected
SPT-CA-08 Acquisition of maximum length address book entries.	as expected
SPT-CA-09 Acquisition of address book entries containing	as expected

Test Case SPT-06 Device Seizure 5.0 build 4582.15907		
	special characters.	
	SPT-CA-10 Acquisition of address book entries containing a blank name entry.	as expected
	SPT-CA-11 Acquisition of embedded email addresses within address book entries.	as expected
	SPT-CA-12 Acquisition of embedded graphics within address book entries.	as expected
	SPT-CA-13 Acquisition of PIM data (i.e., datebook/calendar, notes).	Not as expected
	SPT-CA-14 Acquisition of maximum length PIM data.	as expected
Analysis:	Partial results achieved	

5.2.112 SPT-07 (HTC Thunderbolt)

Test Case SPT-07 Device Seizure 5.0 build 4582.15907	
Case Summary:	SPT-07 Acquire mobile device internal memory and review reported call logs.
Assertions:	SPT-CA-15 If a cellular forensic tool completes acquisition of the target device without error, then call logs (incoming/outgoing/missed) shall be presented in a useable format. SPT-CA-16 If a cellular forensic tool completes acquisition of the target device without error, then the corresponding date/time stamps and the duration of the call for call logs shall be presented in a useable format.
Tester Name:	rpa
Test Host:	Morrisy
Test Date:	Tue Sep 25 11:39:05 EDT 2012
Device:	HTC Thunderbolt
Source Setup:	OS: WIN XP v5.1.2600 Interface: cable
Log Highlights:	Created by Device Seizure v5.0 Acquisition started: Tue Sep 25 11:39:05 EDT 2012 Acquisition finished: Tue Sep 25 12:05:42 EDT 2012 All Call Logs (incoming, outgoing, missed) were acquired All Call Log date/time stamps data were correctly reported
Results:	

Assertion & Expected Result	Actual Result
SPT-CA-15 Acquisition of call logs.	as expected
SPT-CA-16 Acquisition of call log date/time stamps.	as expected

Analysis:	Expected results achieved

5.2.113 SPT-08 (HTC Thunderbolt)

Test Case SPT-08 Device Seizure 5.0 build 4582.15907	
Case Summary:	SPT-08 Acquire mobile device internal memory and review reported text messages.
Assertions:	SPT-CA-17 If a cellular forensic tool completes acquisition of the target device without error, then ASCII text messages (i.e., SMS, EMS) shall be presented in a useable format. SPT-CA-18 If a cellular forensic tool completes acquisition of the target device without error, then the corresponding date/time stamps for text messages shall be presented in a useable format. SPT-CA-19 If a cellular forensic tool completes acquisition of the target device without error, then the corresponding status (i.e., read, unread) for text messages shall be presented in a useable format. SPT-CA-20 If a cellular forensic tool completes acquisition of the target device without error, then the corresponding sender / recipient phone numbers for text messages shall be presented in a useable format.

Test Case SPT-08 Device Seizure 5.0 build 4582.15907	
Tester Name:	rpa
Test Host:	Morrisy
Test Date:	Tue Sep 25 11:40:01 EDT 2012
Device:	HTC Thunderbolt
Source Setup:	OS: WIN XP v5.1.2600 Interface: cable
Log Highlights:	Created by Device Seizure v5.0 Acquisition started: Tue Sep 25 11:40:01 EDT 2012 Acquisition finished: Tue Sep 25 12:06:05 EDT 2012 ALL text messages (SMS, EMS) were acquired Correct date/time stamps were reported for all text messages Correct status flags were reported for all text messages Sender and Recipient phone numbers associated with text messages were correctly reported

Results:	Assertion & Expected Result	Actual Result
	SPT-CA-17 Acquisition of text messages.	as expected
	SPT-CA-18 Acquisition of text message date/time stamps.	as expected
	SPT-CA-19 Acquisition of text message status flags.	as expected
	SPT-CA-20 Acquisition of sender/recipient phone number associated with text messages.	as expected

Analysis:	Expected results achieved

5.2.114 SPT-09 (HTC Thunderbolt)

Test Case SPT-09 Device Seizure 5.0 build 4582.15907	
Case Summary:	SPT-09 Acquire mobile device internal memory and review reported MMS multimedia-related data (i.e., text, audio, graphics, video).
Assertions:	SPT-CA-21 If a cellular forensic tool completes acquisition of the target device without error, then MMS messages and associated audio shall be presented in a useable format. SPT-CA-22 If a cellular forensic tool completes acquisition of the target device without error, then MMS messages and associated graphic files shall be presented in a useable format. SPT-CA-23 If a cellular forensic tool completes acquisition of the target device without error, then MMS messages and associated video shall be presented in a useable format.
Tester Name:	rpa
Test Host:	Morrisy
Test Date:	Tue Sep 25 12:19:14 EDT 2012
Device:	HTC Thunderbolt
Source Setup:	OS: WIN XP v5.1.2600 Interface: cable
Log Highlights:	Created by Device Seizure v5.0 Acquisition started: Tue Sep 25 12:19:14 EDT 2012 Acquisition finished: Tue Sep 25 12:20:08 EDT 2012 ALL MMS messages (Audio, Image, Video) were acquired

Results:	Assertion & Expected Result	Actual Result
	SPT-CA-21 Acquisition of audio MMS messages.	as expected
	SPT-CA-22 Acquisition of graphic data image MMS messages.	as expected
	SPT-CA-23 Acquisition of video MMS messages.	as expected

Test Case SPT-09 Device Seizure 5.0 build 4582.15907	
Analysis:	Expected results achieved

5.2.115 SPT-10 (HTC Thunderbolt)

Test Case SPT-10 Device Seizure 5.0 build 4582.15907	
Case Summary:	SPT-10 Acquire mobile device internal memory and review reported stand-alone multi-media data (i.e., audio, graphics, video).
Assertions:	SPT-CA-24 If a cellular forensic tool completes acquisition of the target device without error, then stand-alone audio files shall be presented in a useable format via either an internal application or suggested third-party application. SPT-CA-25 If a cellular forensic tool completes acquisition of the target device without error, then stand-alone graphic files shall be presented in a useable format via either an internal application or suggested third-party application. SPT-CA-26 If a cellular forensic tool completes acquisition of the target device without error, then stand-alone video files shall be presented in a useable format via either an internal application or suggested third-party application.
Tester Name:	rpa
Test Host:	Morrisy
Test Date:	Tue Sep 25 12:23:27 EDT 2012
Device:	HTC Thunderbolt
Source Setup:	OS: WIN XP v5.1.2600 Interface: cable
Log Highlights:	Created by Device Seizure v5.0 Acquisition started: Tue Sep 25 12:23:27 EDT 2012 Acquisition finished: Tue Sep 25 12:23:41 EDT 2012 Audio files were not acquired Image files were not acquired Video files were not acquired
Results:	

Assertion & Expected Result	Actual Result
SPT-CA-24 Acquisition of stand-alone audio files.	Not as expected
SPT-CA-25 Acquisition of stand-alone graphic files.	Not as expected
SPT-CA-26 Acquisition of stand-alone video files.	Not as expected

Analysis:	Expected results not achieved

5.2.116 SPT-11 (HTC Thunderbolt)

Test Case SPT-11 Device Seizure 5.0 build 4582.15907	
Case Summary:	SPT-11 Acquire mobile device internal memory and review application-related data (i.e., Word documents, spreadsheet, presentation documents).
Assertions:	SPT-CA-27 If a cellular forensic tool completes acquisition of the target device without error, then device specific application-related data shall be acquired and presented in a useable format via either an internal application or suggested third-party application.
Tester Name:	rpa
Test Host:	Morrisy
Test Date:	Tue Sep 25 12:15:39 EDT 2012
Device:	HTC Thunderbolt
Source Setup:	OS: WIN XP v5.1.2600 Interface: cable
Log Highlights:	Created by Device Seizure v5.0 Acquisition started: Tue Sep 25 12:15:39 EDT 2012

Test Case SPT-11 Device Seizure 5.0 build 4582.15907	
	Acquisition finished: Tue Sep 25 12:18:43 EDT 2012 Application data was not acquired
Results:	
	<table><tr><th>Assertion & Expected Result</th><th>Actual Result</th></tr><tr><td>SPT-CA-27 Acquisition of application-related data.</td><td>Not as expected</td></tr></table>
Analysis:	Expected results not achieved

5.2.117 SPT-12 (HTC Thunderbolt)

Test Case SPT-12 Device Seizure 5.0 build 4582.15907	
Case Summary:	SPT-12 Acquire mobile device internal memory and review Internet-related data (i.e., bookmarks, visited sites.
Assertions:	SPT-CA-28 If a cellular forensic tool completes acquisition of the target device without error, then Internet-related data (i.e., bookmarks, visited sites) cached to the device shall be acquired and presented in a useable format.
Tester Name:	rpa
Test Host:	Morrisy
Test Date:	Tue Sep 25 12:11:24 EDT 2012
Device:	HTC Thunderbolt
Source Setup:	OS: WIN XP v5.1.2600 Interface: cable
Log Highlights:	Created by Device Seizure v5.0 Acquisition started: Tue Sep 25 12:11:24 EDT 2012 Acquisition finished: Tue Sep 25 12:11:43 EDT 2012 All Internet-related data was acquired
Results:	
	<table><tr><th>Assertion & Expected Result</th><th>Actual Result</th></tr><tr><td>SPT-CA-28 Acquisition of Internet-related data.</td><td>as expected</td></tr></table>
Analysis:	Expected results achieved

5.2.118 SPT-13 (HTC Thunderbolt)

Test Case SPT-13 Device Seizure 5.0 build 4582.15907	
Case Summary:	SPT-13 Acquire mobile device internal memory by selecting a combination of supported data elements.
Assertions:	SPT-CA-29 If a cellular forensic tool provides the user with an "Acquire All" device data objects acquisition option, then the tool shall complete the acquisition of all data objects without error. SPT-CA-30 If a cellular forensic tool provides the user with an "Select All" individual device data objects, then the tool shall complete the acquisition of all individually selected data objects without error. SPT-CA-31 If a cellular forensic tool provides the user with the ability to "Select Individual" device data objects for acquisition, then the tool shall acquire each exclusive data object without error.
Tester Name:	rpa
Test Host:	Morrisy
Test Date:	Tue Sep 25 12:07:58 EDT 2012
Device:	HTC Thunderbolt
Source Setup:	OS: WIN XP v5.1.2600 Interface: cable
Log Highlights:	Created by Device Seizure v5.0 Acquisition started: Tue Sep 25 12:07:58 EDT 2012

Test Case SPT-13 Device Seizure 5.0 build 4582.15907	
	Acquisition finished: Tue Sep 25 12:11:31 EDT 2012 Acquire All acquisition was successful
Results:	

Assertion & Expected Result	Actual Result
SPT-CA-29 Acquire-All data objects acquisition.	as expected
SPT-CA-30 Select-All data objects acquisition.	as expected
SPT-CA-31 Select-Individual data objects acquisition.	as expected

Analysis:	Expected results achieved

5.2.119 SPT-24 (HTC Thunderbolt)

Test Case SPT-24 Device Seizure 5.0 build 4582.15907	
Case Summary:	SPT-24 Acquire mobile device internal memory and review reported data via supported generated report formats.
Assertions:	SPT-AO-25 If a cellular forensic tool completes acquisition of the target device without error, then the tool shall present the acquired data in a useable format via supported generated report formats.
Tester Name:	rpa
Test Host:	Morrisy
Test Date:	Tue Sep 25 12:24:43 EDT 2012
Device:	HTC Thunderbolt
Source Setup:	OS: WIN XP v5.1.2600 Interface: cable
Log Highlights:	Created by Device Seizure v5.0 Acquisition started: Tue Sep 25 12:24:43 EDT 2012 Acquisition finished: Tue Sep 25 12:38:12 EDT 2012 Complete representation of known data via generated reports was successful
Results:	

Assertion & Expected Result	Actual Result
SPT-AO-25 Comparison of known device data elements via generated reports.	as expected

Analysis:	Expected results achieved

5.2.120 SPT-25 (HTC Thunderbolt)

Test Case SPT-25 Device Seizure 5.0 build 4582.15907	
Case Summary:	SPT-25 Acquire mobile device internal memory and review reported data via the preview pane.
Assertions:	SPT-AO-26 If a cellular forensic tool completes acquisition of the target device without error, then the tool shall present the acquired data in a useable format in a preview pane view.
Tester Name:	rpa
Test Host:	Morrisy
Test Date:	Tue Sep 25 12:24:58 EDT 2012
Device:	HTC Thunderbolt
Source Setup:	OS: WIN XP v5.1.2600 Interface: cable
Log Highlights:	Created by Device Seizure v5.0 Acquisition started: Tue Sep 25 12:24:58 EDT 2012 Acquisition finished: Tue Sep 25 12:38:39 EDT 2012 Complete representation of known data via preview pane was successful

Test Case SPT-25 Device Seizure 5.0 build 4582.15907	
Results:	

Assertion & Expected Result	Actual Result
SPT-AO-26 Comparison of known device data elements via preview pane.	as expected

Analysis:	Expected results achieved

5.2.121 SPT-29 (HTC Thunderbolt)

Test Case SPT-29 Device Seizure 5.0 build 4582.15907	
Case Summary:	SPT-29 After a successful mobile device internal memory, alter the case file via third-party means and attempt to reopen the case.
Assertions:	SPT-AO-27 If the case file or individual data objects are modified via third-party means, then the tool shall provide protection mechanisms disallowing or reporting data modification.
Tester Name:	rpa
Test Host:	Morrisy
Test Date:	Tue Sep 25 12:25:32 EDT 2012
Device:	HTC_Thunderbolt
Source Setup:	OS: WIN XP v5.1.2600 Interface: cable
Log Highlights:	Created by Device Seizure v5.0 Acquisition started: Tue Sep 25 12:25:32 EDT 2012 Acquisition finished: Tue Sep 25 12:26:33 EDT 2012 Notification of modified device memory data was successful
Results:	

Assertion & Expected Result	Actual Result
SPT-AO-27 Notification of modified device case data.	as expected

Analysis:	Expected results achieved

5.2.122 SPT-33 (HTC Thunderbolt)

Test Case SPT-33 Device Seizure 5.0 build 4582.15907	
Case Summary:	SPT-33 Acquire mobile device internal memory and review data containing non-ASCII characters.
Assertions:	SPT-AO-40 If the cellular forensic tool supports display of non-ASCII characters, then the application should present address book entries in their native format. SPT-AO-41 If the cellular forensic tool supports proper display of non-ASCII characters, then the application should present text messages in their native format.
Tester Name:	rpa
Test Host:	Morrisy
Test Date:	Tue Sep 25 12:25:47 EDT 2012
Device:	HTC Thunderbolt
Source Setup:	OS: WIN XP v5.1.2600 Interface: cable
Log Highlights:	Created by Device Seizure v5.0 Acquisition started: Tue Sep 25 12:25:47 EDT 2012 Acquisition finished: Tue Sep 25 12:26:47 EDT 2012 Non-ASCII Address book entries were acquired and properly displayed Non-ASCII text messages were acquired and properly displayed

Test Case SPT-33 Device Seizure 5.0 build 4582.15907		
Results:		
	Assertion & Expected Result	**Actual Result**
	SPT-AO-40 Acquisition of non-ASCII address book entries/ADNs.	as expected
	SPT-AO-41 Acquisition of non-ASCII text messages.	as expected
Analysis:	Expected results achieved	

5.2.123 SPT-38 (HTC Thunderbolt)

Test Case SPT-38 Device Seizure 5.0 build 4582.15907	
Case Summary:	SPT-38 Acquire mobile device internal memory and review hash values for vendor supported data objects.
Assertions:	SPT-AO-43 If the cellular forensic tool supports hashing for individual data objects, then the tool shall present the user with a hash value for each supported data object.
Tester Name:	rpa
Test Host:	Morrisy
Test Date:	Tue Sep 25 12:26:05 EDT 2012
Device:	HTC_Thunderbolt
Source Setup:	OS: WIN XP v5.1.2600 Interface: cable
Log Highlights:	Created by Device Seizure v5.0 Acquisition started: Tue Sep 25 12:26:05 EDT 2012 Acquisition finished: Tue Sep 25 12:27:02 EDT 2012 Hash values were properly reported for individually acquired device data elements
Results:	

	Assertion & Expected Result	**Actual Result**
	SPT-AO-43 Acquire data, check known hash values for consistency.	as expected

Analysis:	Expected results achieved

5.2.124 SPT-01 (Palm Pre2)

Test Case SPT-01 Device Seizure 5.0 build 4582.15907	
Case Summary:	SPT-01 Acquire mobile device internal memory over tool-supported interfaces (e.g., cable, Bluetooth, IrDA).
Assertions:	SPT-CA-01 If a cellular forensic tool provides support for connectivity of the target device, then the tool shall successfully recognize the target device via all vendor supported interfaces (e.g., cable, Bluetooth, IrDA). SPT-CA-04 If a cellular forensic tool completes acquisition of the target device without error, then the tool shall have the ability to present acquired data objects in a useable format via either a preview pane or generated report. SPT-CA-29 If a cellular forensic tool provides the user with an "Acquire All" device data objects acquisition option, then the tool shall complete the acquisition of all data objects without error. SPT-CA-30 If a cellular forensic tool provides the user with a "Select All" individual device data objects, then the tool shall complete the acquisition of all individually selected data objects without error. SPT-CA-31 If a cellular forensic tool provides the user with the ability to "Select Individual" device data objects for acquisition, then the tool shall acquire each exclusive data object without error. SPT-CA-32 If a cellular forensic tool completes two consecutive logical acquisitions of the target device without error, then the payload (data

Test Case SPT-01 Device Seizure 5.0 build 4582.15907	
	objects) on the mobile device shall remain consistent.
Tester Name:	rpa
Test Host:	Morrisy
Test Date:	Tue Sep 25 12:54:19 EDT 2012
Device:	Palm Pre2
Source Setup:	OS: WIN XP v5.1.2600 Interface: cable
Log Highlights:	Created by Device Seizure v5.0 Acquisition started: Tue Sep 25 12:54:19 EDT 2012 Acquisition finished: Tue Sep 25 12:57:24 EDT 2012 Device connectivity was established via supported interface
Results:	

Assertion & Expected Result	Actual Result
SPT-CA-01 Device connectivity via supported interfaces.	as expected
SPT-CA-04 Readability and completeness of acquired data via supported reports.	as expected
SPT-CA-29 Acquire-All data objects acquisition.	as expected
SPT-CA-30 Select-All data objects acquisition.	as expected
SPT-CA-31 Select-Individual data objects acquisition.	as expected
SPT-CA-32 Perform back-to-back acquisitions, check device payload for modifications.	as expected

Analysis:	Expected results achieved

5.2.125 SPT-02 (Palm Pre2)

Test Case SPT-02 Device Seizure 5.0 build 4582.15907	
Case Summary:	SPT-02 Attempt internal memory acquisition of a nonsupported mobile device.
Assertions:	SPT-CA-02 If a cellular forensic tool attempts to connect to a nonsupported device, then the tool shall notify the user that the device is not supported.
Tester Name:	rpa
Test Host:	Morrisy
Test Date:	Tue Sep 25 12:54:43 EDT 2012
Device:	Palm Pre2
Source Setup:	OS: WIN XP v5.1.2600 Interface: cable
Log Highlights:	Created by Device Seizure v5.0 Acquisition started: Tue Sep 25 12:54:43 EDT 2012 Acquisition finished: Tue Sep 25 12:57:34 EDT 2012 Identification of nonsupported devices was successful
Results:	

Assertion & Expected Result	Actual Result
SPT-CA-02 Identification of nonsupported devices.	as expected

Analysis:	Expected results achieved

5.2.126 SPT-03 (Palm Pre2)

Test Case SPT-03 Device Seizure 5.0 build 4582.15907	
Case Summary:	SPT-03 Begin mobile device internal memory acquisition and interrupt connectivity by interface disengagement.

Test Case SPT-03 Device Seizure 5.0 build 4582.15907	
Assertions:	SPT-CA-03 If connectivity between the mobile device and cellular forensic tool is disrupted, then the tool shall notify the user that connectivity has been disrupted.
Tester Name:	rpa
Test Host:	Morrisy
Test Date:	Tue Sep 25 12:55:01 EDT 2012
Device:	Palm_Pre2
Source Setup:	OS: WIN XP v5.1.2600 Interface: cable
Log Highlights:	Created by Device Seizure v5.0 Acquisition started: Tue Sep 25 12:55:01 EDT 2012 Acquisition finished: Tue Sep 25 12:57:46 EDT 2012 Device acquisition disruption notification was successful

Results:		
	Assertion & Expected Result	**Actual Result**
	SPT-CA-03 Notification of device acquisition disruption.	as expected

Analysis:	Expected results achieved

5.2.127 SPT-04 (Palm Pre2)

Test Case SPT-04 Device Seizure 5.0 build 4582.15907	
Case Summary:	SPT-04 Acquire mobile device internal memory and review reported data via the preview pane or generated reports for readability.
Assertions:	SPT-CA-04 If a cellular forensic tool completes acquisition of the target device without error, then the tool shall have the ability to present acquired data objects in a useable format via either a preview pane or generated report.
Tester Name:	rpa
Test Host:	Morrisy
Test Date:	Tue Sep 25 13:04:35 EDT 2012
Device:	Palm_Pre2
Source Setup:	OS: WIN XP v5.1.2600 Interface: cable
Log Highlights:	Created by Device Seizure v5.0 Acquisition started: Tue Sep 25 13:04:35 EDT 2012 Acquisition finished: Tue Sep 25 13:08:57 EDT 2012 Readability and completeness of acquired data was successful

Results:		
	Assertion & Expected Result	**Actual Result**
	SPT-CA-04 Readability and completeness of acquired data via supported reports.	as expected

Analysis:	Expected results achieved

5.2.128 SPT-05 (Palm Pre2)

Test Case SPT-05 Device Seizure 5.0 build 4582.15907	
Case Summary:	SPT-05 Acquire mobile device internal memory and review reported subscriber and equipment-related information (e.g., IMEI/MEID/ESN, MSISDN).
Assertions:	SPT-CA-05 If a cellular forensic tool completes acquisition of the target device without error, then subscriber related information shall be presented in a useable format.

Test Case SPT-05 Device Seizure 5.0 build 4582.15907	
	SPT-CA-06 If a cellular forensic tool completes acquisition of the target device without error, then equipment-related information shall be presented in a useable format.
Tester Name:	rpa
Test Host:	Morrisy
Test Date:	Tue Sep 25 13:09:51 EDT 2012
Device:	Palm Pre2
Source Setup:	OS: WIN XP v5.1.2600 Interface: cable
Log Highlights:	Created by Device Seizure v5.0 Acquisition started: Tue Sep 25 13:09:51 EDT 2012 Acquisition finished: Tue Sep 25 13:44:25 EDT 2012 IMEI, MEID/ESN were not acquired
Results:	

Assertion & Expected Result	Actual Result
SPT-CA-05 Acquisition of MSISDN, IMSI.	Not as expected
SPT-CA-06 Acquisition of IMEI/MEID/ESN.	Not as expected

Analysis:	Expected results not achieved

5.2.129 SPT-06 (Palm Pre2)

Test Case SPT-06 Device Seizure 5.0 build 4582.15907	
Case Summary:	SPT-06 Acquire mobile device internal memory and review reported PIM-related data.
Assertions:	SPT-CA-07 If a cellular forensic tool completes acquisition of the target device without error, then address book entries shall be presented in a useable format. SPT-CA-08 If a cellular forensic tool completes acquisition of the target device without error, then maximum length address book entries shall be presented in a useable format. SPT-CA-09 If a cellular forensic tool completes acquisition of the target device without error, then address book entries containing special characters shall be presented in a useable format. SPT-CA-10 If a cellular forensic tool completes acquisition of the target device without error, then address book entries containing blank names shall be presented in a useable format. SPT-CA-11 If a cellular forensic tool completes acquisition of the target device without error, then email addresses associated with address book entries shall be presented in a useable format. SPT-CA-12 If a cellular forensic tool completes acquisition of the target device without error, then graphics associated with address book entries shall be presented in a useable format. SPT-CA-13 If a cellular forensic tool completes acquisition of the target device without error, then datebook, calendar, note entries shall be presented in a useable format. SPT-CA-14 If a cellular forensic tool completes acquisition of the target device without error, then maximum length datebook, calendar, note entries shall be presented in a useable format.
Tester Name:	rpa
Test Host:	Morrisy
Test Date:	Tue Sep 25 13:10:07 EDT 2012
Device:	Palm Pre2
Source Setup:	OS: WIN XP v5.1.2600 Interface: cable
Log Highlights:	Created by Device Seizure v5.0 Acquisition started: Tue Sep 25 13:10:07 EDT 2012 Acquisition finished: Tue Sep 25 13:44:47 EDT 2012 Regular Length Address Book entries were not acquired

Test Case SPT-06 Device Seizure 5.0 build 4582.15907		
	Maximum Length Address Book entries were not acquired Special Character Address Book entries were not acquired Blank Name Address Book entries were not acquired Email addresses within Address Book entries were not acquired Embedded graphics within Address Book entries were not acquired Basic PIM-related data was not acquired Maximum length PIM-related data was not acquired	
Results:		

Assertion & Expected Result	Actual Result
SPT-CA-07 Acquisition of address book entries.	Not as expected
SPT-CA-08 Acquisition of maximum length address book entries.	NA
SPT-CA-09 Acquisition of address book entries containing special characters.	NA
SPT-CA-10 Acquisition of address book entries containing a blank name entry.	NA
SPT-CA-11 Acquisition of embedded email addresses within address book entries.	NA
SPT-CA-12 Acquisition of embedded graphics within address book entries.	NA
SPT-CA-13 Acquisition of PIM data (i.e., datebook/calendar, notes).	Not as expected
SPT-CA-14 Acquisition of maximum length PIM data.	NA

Analysis:	Expected results not achieved

5.2.130 SPT-07 (Palm Pre2)

Test Case SPT-07 Device Seizure 5.0 build 4582.15907	
Case Summary:	SPT-07 Acquire mobile device internal memory and review reported call logs.
Assertions:	SPT-CA-15 If a cellular forensic tool completes acquisition of the target device without error, then call logs (incoming/outgoing/missed) shall be presented in a useable format. SPT-CA-16 If a cellular forensic tool completes acquisition of the target device without error, then the corresponding date/time stamps and the duration of the call for call logs shall be presented in a useable format.
Tester Name:	rpa
Test Host:	Morrisy
Test Date:	Tue Sep 25 13:10:27 EDT 2012
Device:	
Source Setup:	OS: WIN XP v5.1.2600 Interface: cable
Log Highlights:	Created by Device Seizure v5.0 Acquisition started: Tue Sep 25 13:10:27 EDT 2012 Acquisition finished: Tue Sep 25 13:45:09 EDT 2012 Incoming Calls were not acquired Outgoing Calls were not acquired Missed Calls were not acquired Date/Time Stamps incorrectly reported for Incoming Calls Date/Time Stamps incorrectly reported for Outgoing Calls Date/Time Stamps incorrectly reported for Missed Calls
Results:	

Assertion & Expected Result	Actual Result
SPT-CA-15 Acquisition of call logs.	Not as expected
SPT-CA-16 Acquisition of call log date/time stamps.	Not as expected

Analysis:	Expected results not achieved

5.2.131 SPT-08 (Palm Pre2)

Test Case SPT-08 Device Seizure 5.0 build 4582.15907	
Case Summary:	SPT-08 Acquire mobile device internal memory and review reported text messages.
Assertions:	SPT-CA-17 If a cellular forensic tool completes acquisition of the target device without error, then ASCII text messages (i.e., SMS, EMS) shall be presented in a useable format. SPT-CA-18 If a cellular forensic tool completes acquisition of the target device without error, then the corresponding date/time stamps for text messages shall be presented in a useable format. SPT-CA-19 If a cellular forensic tool completes acquisition of the target device without error, then the corresponding status (i.e., read, unread) for text messages shall be presented in a useable format. SPT-CA-20 If a cellular forensic tool completes acquisition of the target device without error, then the corresponding sender / recipient phone numbers for text messages shall be presented in a useable format.
Tester Name:	rpa
Test Host:	Morrisy
Test Date:	Tue Sep 25 13:10:42 EDT 2012
Device:	Palm Pre2
Source Setup:	OS: WIN XP v5.1.2600 Interface: cable
Log Highlights:	Created by Device Seizure v5.0 Acquisition started: Tue Sep 25 13:10:42 EDT 2012 Acquisition finished: Tue Sep 25 13:45:33 EDT 2012 Text messages were not acquired Incorrect status flags were reported for text messages Sender and Recipient phone numbers associated with text messages were incorrectly reported

Results:	Assertion & Expected Result	Actual Result
	SPT-CA-17 Acquisition of text messages.	Not as expected
	SPT-CA-18 Acquisition of text message date/time stamps.	NA
	SPT-CA-19 Acquisition of text message status flags.	NA
	SPT-CA-20 Acquisition of sender/recipient phone number associated with text messages.	NA

Analysis:	Expected results not achieved

5.2.132 SPT-09 (Palm Pre2)

Test Case SPT-09 Device Seizure 5.0 build 4582.15907	
Case Summary:	SPT-09 Acquire mobile device internal memory and review reported MMS multi-media-related data (i.e., text, audio, graphics, video).
Assertions:	SPT-CA-21 If a cellular forensic tool completes acquisition of the target device without error, then MMS messages and associated audio shall be presented in a useable format. SPT-CA-22 If a cellular forensic tool completes acquisition of the target device without error, then MMS messages and associated graphic files shall be presented in a useable format. SPT-CA-23 If a cellular forensic tool completes acquisition of the target device without error, then MMS messages and associated video shall be presented in a useable format.
Tester Name:	rpa
Test Host:	Morrisy
Test Date:	Tue Sep 25 13:11:04 EDT 2012

Test Case SPT-09 Device Seizure 5.0 build 4582.15907	
Device:	Palm_Pre2
Source Setup:	OS: WIN XP v5.1.2600 Interface: cable
Log Highlights:	Created by Device Seizure v5.0 Acquisition started: Tue Sep 25 13:11:04 EDT 2012 Acquisition finished: Tue Sep 25 13:45:51 EDT 2012 Audio MMS messages were not acquired Image MMS messages were not acquired Video MMS messages were not acquired
Results:	

Assertion & Expected Result	Actual Result
SPT-CA-21 Acquisition of audio MMS messages.	Not as expected
SPT-CA-22 Acquisition of graphic data image MMS messages.	Not as expected
SPT-CA-23 Acquisition of video MMS messages.	Not as expected

Analysis:	Expected results not achieved

5.2.133 SPT-10 (Palm Pre2)

Test Case SPT-10 Device Seizure 5.0 build 4582.15907	
Case Summary:	SPT-10 Acquire mobile device internal memory and review reported stand-alone multi-media data (i.e., audio, graphics, video).
Assertions:	SPT-CA-24 If a cellular forensic tool completes acquisition of the target device without error, then stand-alone audio files shall be presented in a useable format via either an internal application or suggested third-party application. SPT-CA-25 If a cellular forensic tool completes acquisition of the target device without error, then stand-alone graphic files shall be presented in a useable format via either an internal application or suggested third-party application. SPT-CA-26 If a cellular forensic tool completes acquisition of the target device without error, then stand-alone video files shall be presented in a useable format via either an internal application or suggested third-party application.
Tester Name:	rpa
Test Host:	Morrisy
Test Date:	Tue Sep 25 13:11:19 EDT 2012
Device:	Palm_Pre2
Source Setup:	OS: WIN XP v5.1.2600 Interface: cable
Log Highlights:	Created by Device Seizure v5.0 Acquisition started: Tue Sep 25 13:11:19 EDT 2012 Acquisition finished: Tue Sep 25 13:46:06 EDT 2012 Audio files were not acquired Image files were not acquired Video files were not acquired
Results:	

Assertion & Expected Result	Actual Result
SPT-CA-24 Acquisition of stand-alone audio files.	Not as expected
SPT-CA-25 Acquisition of stand-alone graphic files.	Not as expected
SPT-CA-26 Acquisition of stand-alone video files.	Not as expected

Analysis:	Expected results not achieved

5.2.134 SPT-11 (Palm Pre2)

Test Case SPT-11 Device Seizure 5.0 build 4582.15907	
Case Summary:	SPT-11 Acquire mobile device internal memory and review application-related data (i.e., Word documents, spreadsheet, presentation documents).
Assertions:	SPT-CA-27 If a cellular forensic tool completes acquisition of the target device without error, then device specific application-related data shall be acquired and presented in a useable format via either an internal application or suggested third-party application.
Tester Name:	rpa
Test Host:	Morrisy
Test Date:	Tue Sep 25 13:12:05 EDT 2012
Device:	Palm Pre2
Source Setup:	OS: WIN XP v5.1.2600 Interface: cable
Log Highlights:	Created by Device Seizure v5.0 Acquisition started: Tue Sep 25 13:12:05 EDT 2012 Acquisition finished: Tue Sep 25 13:46:21 EDT 2012 Application data was not acquired
Results:	

Assertion & Expected Result	Actual Result
SPT-CA-27 Acquisition of application-related data.	Not as expected

Analysis:	Expected results not achieved

5.2.135 SPT-12 (Palm Pre2)

Test Case SPT-12 Device Seizure 5.0 build 4582.15907	
Case Summary:	SPT-12 Acquire mobile device internal memory and review Internet-related data (i.e., bookmarks, visited sites.
Assertions:	SPT-CA-28 If a cellular forensic tool completes acquisition of the target device without error, then Internet-related data (i.e., bookmarks, visited sites) cached to the device shall be acquired and presented in a useable format.
Tester Name:	rpa
Test Host:	Morrisy
Test Date:	Tue Sep 25 13:12:21 EDT 2012
Device:	Palm Pre2
Source Setup:	OS: WIN XP v5.1.2600 Interface: cable
Log Highlights:	Created by Device Seizure v5.0 Acquisition started: Tue Sep 25 13:12:21 EDT 2012 Acquisition finished: Tue Sep 25 13:46:34 EDT 2012 Internet-related data was not acquired
Results:	

Assertion & Expected Result	Actual Result
SPT-CA-28 Acquisition of Internet-related data.	Not as expected

Analysis:	Expected results not achieved

5.2.136 SPT-13 (Palm Pre2)

Test Case SPT-13 Device Seizure 5.0 build 4582.15907	
Case Summary:	SPT-13 Acquire mobile device internal memory by selecting a combination of supported data elements.

Test Case SPT-13 Device Seizure 5.0 build 4582.15907	
Assertions:	SPT-CA-29 If a cellular forensic tool provides the user with an "Acquire All" device data objects acquisition option, then the tool shall complete the acquisition of all data objects without error. SPT-CA-30 If a cellular forensic tool provides the user with an "Select All" individual device data objects, then the tool shall complete the acquisition of all individually selected data objects without error. SPT-CA-31 If a cellular forensic tool provides the user with the ability to "Select Individual" device data objects for acquisition, then the tool shall acquire each exclusive data object without error.
Tester Name:	rpa
Test Host:	Morrisy
Test Date:	Tue Sep 25 13:03:12 EDT 2012
Device:	Palm Pre2
Source Setup:	OS: WIN XP v5.1.2600 Interface: cable
Log Highlights:	Created by Device Seizure v5.0 Acquisition started: Tue Sep 25 13:03:12 EDT 2012 Acquisition finished: Tue Sep 25 13:03:56 EDT 2012 Acquire All acquisition was successful
Results:	

Assertion & Expected Result	Actual Result
SPT-CA-29 Acquire-All data objects acquisition.	as expected
SPT-CA-30 Select-All data objects acquisition.	as expected
SPT-CA-31 Select-Individual data objects acquisition.	as expected

Analysis:	Expected results achieved

5.2.137 SPT-24 (Palm Pre2)

Test Case SPT-24 Device Seizure 5.0 build 4582.15907	
Case Summary:	SPT-24 Acquire mobile device internal memory and review reported data via supported generated report formats.
Assertions:	SPT-AO-25 If a cellular forensic tool completes acquisition of the target device without error, then the tool shall present the acquired data in a useable format via supported generated report formats.
Tester Name:	rpa
Test Host:	Morrisy
Test Date:	Tue Sep 25 12:58:22 EDT 2012
Device:	Palm Pre2
Source Setup:	OS: WIN XP v5.1.2600 Interface: cable
Log Highlights:	Created by Device Seizure v5.0 Acquisition started: Tue Sep 25 12:58:22 EDT 2012 Acquisition finished: Tue Sep 25 13:00:47 EDT 2012 Complete representation of known data via generated reports was successful
Results:	

Assertion & Expected Result	Actual Result
SPT-AO-25 Comparison of known device data elements via generated reports.	as expected

Analysis:	Expected results achieved

5.2.138 SPT-25 (Palm Pre2)

Test Case SPT-25 Device Seizure 5.0 build 4582.15907	
Case Summary:	SPT-25 Acquire mobile device internal memory and review reported data via the preview pane.
Assertions:	SPT-AO-26 If a cellular forensic tool completes acquisition of the target device without error, then the tool shall present the acquired data in a useable format in a preview pane view.
Tester Name:	rpa
Test Host:	Morrisy
Test Date:	Tue Sep 25 12:58:37 EDT 2012
Device:	Palm Pre2
Source Setup:	OS: WIN XP v5.1.2600 Interface: cable
Log Highlights:	Created by Device Seizure v5.0 Acquisition started: Tue Sep 25 12:58:37 EDT 2012 Acquisition finished: Tue Sep 25 13:01:02 EDT 2012 Complete representation of known data via preview pane was successful

Results:		
	Assertion & Expected Result	**Actual Result**
	SPT-AO-26 Comparison of known device data elements via preview pane.	as expected

Analysis:	Expected results achieved

5.2.139 SPT-29 (Palm Pre2)

Test Case SPT-29 Device Seizure 5.0 build 4582.15907	
Case Summary:	SPT-29 After a successful mobile device internal memory, alter the case file via third-party means and attempt to reopen the case.
Assertions:	SPT-AO-27 If the case file or individual data objects are modified via third-party means, then the tool shall provide protection mechanisms disallowing or reporting data modification.
Tester Name:	rpa
Test Host:	Morrisy
Test Date:	Tue Sep 25 13:02:26 EDT 2012
Device:	Palm Pre2
Source Setup:	OS: WIN XP v5.1.2600 Interface: cable
Log Highlights:	Created by Device Seizure v5.0 Acquisition started: Tue Sep 25 13:02:26 EDT 2012 Acquisition finished: Tue Sep 25 13:03:20 EDT 2012 Notification of modified device memory data was successful

Results:		
	Assertion & Expected Result	**Actual Result**
	SPT-AO-27 Notification of modified device case data.	as expected

Analysis:	Expected results achieved

5.2.140 SPT-38 (Palm Pre2)

Test Case SPT-38 Device Seizure 5.0 build 4582.15907	
Case Summary:	SPT-38 Acquire mobile device internal memory and review hash values for vendor supported data objects.
Assertions:	SPT-AO-43 If the cellular forensic tool supports hashing for individual

Test Case SPT-38 Device Seizure 5.0 build 4582.15907	
	data objects, then the tool shall present the user with a hash value for each supported data object.
Tester Name:	rpa
Test Host:	Morrisy
Test Date:	Tue Sep 25 13:02:47 EDT 2012
Device:	Palm Pre2
Source Setup:	OS: WIN XP v5.1.2600 Interface: cable
Log Highlights:	Created by Device Seizure v5.0 Acquisition started: Tue Sep 25 13:02:47 EDT 2012 Acquisition finished: Tue Sep 25 13:03:35 EDT 2012 Hash values were properly reported for individually acquired device data elements

Results:		
	Assertion & Expected Result	Actual Result
	SPT-AO-43 Acquire data, check known hash values for consistency.	as expected

Analysis:	Expected results achieved

About the National Institute of Justice

A component of the Office of Justice Programs, NIJ is the research, development and evaluation agency of the U.S. Department of Justice. NIJ's mission is to advance scientific research, development and evaluation to enhance the administration of justice and public safety. NIJ's principal authorities are derived from the Omnibus Crime Control and Safe Streets Act of 1968, as amended (see 42 U.S.C. §§ 3721–3723).

The NIJ Director is appointed by the President and confirmed by the Senate. The Director establishes the Institute's objectives, guided by the priorities of the Office of Justice Programs, the U.S. Department of Justice, and the needs of the field. The Institute actively solicits the views of criminal justice and other professionals and researchers to inform its search for the knowledge and tools to guide policy and practice.

Strategic Goals

NIJ has seven strategic goals grouped into three categories:

Creating relevant knowledge and tools

1. Partner with state and local practitioners and policymakers to identify social science research and technology needs.
2. Create scientific, relevant, and reliable knowledge—with a particular emphasis on terrorism, violent crime, drugs and crime, cost-effectiveness, and community-based efforts—to enhance the administration of justice and public safety.
3. Develop affordable and effective tools and technologies to enhance the administration of justice and public safety.

Dissemination

4. Disseminate relevant knowledge and information to practitioners and policymakers in an understandable, timely and concise manner.
5. Act as an honest broker to identify the information, tools and technologies that respond to the needs of stakeholders.

Agency management

6. Practice fairness and openness in the research and development process.
7. Ensure professionalism, excellence, accountability, cost-effectiveness and integrity in the management and conduct of NIJ activities and programs.

Program Areas

In addressing these strategic challenges, the Institute is involved in the following program areas: crime control and prevention, including policing; drugs and crime; justice systems and offender behavior, including corrections; violence and victimization; communications and information technologies; critical incident response; investigative and forensic sciences, including DNA; less-than-lethal technologies; officer protection; education and training technologies; testing and standards; technology assistance to law enforcement and corrections agencies; field testing of promising programs; and international crime control.

In addition to sponsoring research and development and technology assistance, NIJ evaluates programs, policies, and technologies. NIJ communicates its research and evaluation findings through conferences and print and electronic media.

To find out more about the National Institute of Justice, please visit:

www.nij.gov

or contact:

National Criminal Justice
  Reference Service
P.O. Box 6000
Rockville, MD 20849–6000
800–851–3420
http://www.ncjrs.gov